About The Reader

The Reader magazine is published by **The Reader**, a not-for-profit organisation within the University of Liverpool. The organisation has grown out of the magazine, which was launched when the founder editors were literature teachers in the Continuing Education programme. In what seemed a unique community, free from the constraints of exams or accreditation, readers aged 18–80 and from all educational backgrounds were sharing reading difficulties and enthusiasms. There was a sense of exhilaration: we were reading big and daunting works together with growing confidence. The desire to keep that spirit alive is behind everything we do.

The Reader magazine first appeared in 1997. We continue to provide a platform for personal and passionate responses to books, as well as seeking to identify new and exciting writers. We also publish a free newsletter which details our events and projects.

Events include **Readers' Days**, where people from all walks of life come together to discuss books, stories and poems; large-scale public events like the **Penny Readings**, which look to recreate the meetings where Dickens would read to thousands; and live events featuring authors as diverse as David Constantine, Doris Lessing and Will Self. **The Reader** also offers tailored training for organisations that wish to put reading into the heart of their work.

The Reader's participation programme, **Get into Reading**, is our largest area of work, actively seeking out new readers in non-traditional or disadvantaged areas. We believe that literature has a purpose in the world beyond the syllabus, classroom or lecture hall, and that its absence from common life is a loss to be remedied. We set up weekly reading groups where facilitators read aloud, ensuring that the words are made real for readers and non-readers alike. This makes a **Get Into Reading** group profoundly democratic and leaves the power – to join in and to speak, or to remain silent and private – entirely with the individual. Group members report increased confidence, concentration and motivation.

The Reader

No. 22, Summer 2006

Address The Reader
19 Abercromby Square
Liverpool L69 7ZG

Email readers@liverpool.ac.uk
Website www.thereader.co.uk

Subscriptions see p. 119
Cover picture by Emma Raynes

ISBN 0-9551168-1-3
978-0-9551168-1-0
Distribution information p. 128

Submissions

The Reader welcomes submissions of poetry, fiction, essays, readings and thought. We publish professional writers and absolute beginners with emphasis on quality and originality of voice. Send your manuscript to: The Reader Office, 19 Abercromby Sq., Liverpool L69 7ZG, UK. **New York Office,** Enid Stubin, 200 East 24th St., Apt. 504, New York, NY, 10010. SAE with all manuscripts please.

Published by The University of Liverpool School of English.
Supported by:

THE UNIVERSITY of LIVERPOOL

ARTS COUNCIL ENGLAND

friends OF THE UNIVERSITY OF LIVERPOOL

Printed and bound in the European Union
by Bell and Bain Ltd, Glasgow

contents

Look out in this issue for quotations from John Donne's poems and Dostoevsky, *The Brothers Karamazov*.

Tell Me a Story

Jane Davis

The Johnny Cash biopic *Walk the Line* quickened memories of my childhood in Toxteth, Liverpool. My mother, a divorcee with four young children, had taken a pub so as to make a living without having to go out to work. On the corner of an early Victorian street behind the looming and unfinished Anglican Cathedral, in an area still marked, in 1968, by wartime bomb-damage, our pub The Little House consisted of a tiny L-shaped bar and an even tinier wedge-shaped parlour. Stairs behind the bar led up directly into our living room. Around us the old terraces were being demolished and their occupants shunted to homes on the new outlying estates. But on Friday and Saturday nights, under my mother's regime, the pub was full of regulars living as if there were no tomorrow. She bought a record player from a customer (an act for which she was eventually tried: 'receiving stolen goods') and set it up on the bar, encouraging everyone to bring in their favourite records.

At first, in this world, I was a talking point because I went to 'College' (the local grammar school) *and wore a hat to school* but generally, in our street, education counted for little: natural talents made you great: a singing voice, beauty, being hard, good at snooker or having a poker face. Alex, a long-haired sailor, was admired for his ability to recite what seemed books of poetry by someone called John Donne but our admiration was of the sort we might have reserved for an African Grey Parrot preaching from Genesis in the original Hebrew: it seemed an amazing feat of training and memory ('all those hours on board with nothing to do…' explained my mother) but it carried the potential for creating boredom in the audience, irritation even, as for all Alex's soulful expression, it was mostly meaningless to us. We didn't rate his John Donne half as much as Barbara's ability to belt out 'The Birth of The Blues' when she'd had enough gin and orange. But the greatest natural gift, universally admired, even in an ugly woman, was narrative wit: the ability to tell a good story. So when Johnny Cash's LP *Live at Folsom Prison* appeared in the bar, everyone fell in love. He was a poet, and he was singing our stories:

> When I was just a baby my mama told me, Son,
> Always be a good boy, don't ever play with guns.

> But I shot a man in Reno just to watch him die
> Now every time I hear that whistle I hang my head
> and cry…

A story doesn't have to be true or an exact fit to work its magic, but it does need to map truly onto certain touchpoints. Probably no one in The Little House had 'shot a man in Reno' but at the heart of these songs was struggle, hardship, sweet-and-sour love, above all, the creative ability to make something out of pain, and these things made Johnny Cash speak to and for us.

The instinct for narrative is strong and so deep, perhaps, as to be rooted in the very structures of consciousness. We experience both an inner and an outer world and we seem hardwired to seek ways of moving between the two states: stories bring the inside out, take the outside in, and something about that experience is both spellbinding and vital. That is the individual experience of narrative function but, beyond that, communal story-sharing *creates* community, and extends personal relationships into the public sphere. Dickens knew this, which is one reason why he took so much pleasure in public readings. The direct effect on his audience was something which thrilled him and connected to the deep sources of his writing:

> Whatever brings a public man and his public face to face is a good thing… a tried means of strengthening those relations, I may almost say of personal friendship, which it is my great privilege and pride, as it is my great responsibility, to hold with a multitude of persons who will never hear my voice or see my face.

The Dickens model of reading, whether live or on the page, is one of 'personal friendship': he's a man speaking the language of men, the only language, in his estimation, worth using. Here, in a passage from *Bleak House*, is Dickens on the subject of 'reader development' as practised by the do-gooder Mrs Pardiggle, when she goes to 'do good' with books in the bricklayer's cottage:

> Besides ourselves, there were in this damp, offensive room a woman with a black eye, nursing a poor little gasping baby by the fire; a man, all stained with clay and mud and looking very dissipated, lying at full length on the ground, smoking a pipe; a powerful young man fastening a collar on a dog; and a bold girl doing some kind of washing in very dirty water. They all looked up at us as we came in, and the woman seemed to turn her face towards the fire as if to hide her bruised eye; nobody gave

> us any welcome [...]
>
> 'You can't tire me, good people,' said Mrs. Pardiggle. 'I enjoy hard work, and the harder you make mine, the better I like it.'
>
> 'Then make it easy for her!' growled the man upon the floor. 'I wants it done, and over. I wants an end of these liberties took with my place. I wants an end of being drawed like a badger. Now you're a-going to poll-pry and question according to custom – I know what you're a-going to be up to. Well! You haven't got no occasion to be up to it. I'll save you the trouble. Is my daughter a-washin? Yes, she IS a-washin. Look at the water. Smell it! That's wot we drinks. How do you like it, and what do you think of gin instead! An't my place dirty? Yes, it is dirty – it's nat'rally dirty, and it's nat'rally onwholesome; and we've had five dirty and onwholesome children, as is all dead infants, and so much the better for them, and for us besides. Have I read the little book wot you left? No, I an't read the little book wot you left. There an't nobody here as knows how to read it; and if there wos, it wouldn't be suitable to me. It's a book fit for a babby, and I'm not a babby. If you was to leave me a doll, I shouldn't nuss it. How have I been conducting of myself? Why, I've been drunk for three days; and I'da been drunk four if I'da had the money. Don't I never mean for to go to church? No, I don't never mean for to go to church. I shouldn't be expected there, if I did; the beadle's too gen-teel for me. And how did my wife get that black eye? Why, I give it her; and if she says I didn't, she's a lie!'

The little book 'fit for a babby' is unsuitable for the brickmaker because it reflects nothing of the complex and terrible life he knows – and the difference, as he intelligently intuits, is one of reality: 'if you was to leave me a doll I shouldn't nuss it', says the grown man who has buried five children. The little book ain't real.

In *Walk the Line*, John and his older brother discuss the merits of their likely careers, singer and preacher. John bows to his brother's learning, saying something like: 'You know every story in the Bible' and his brother shrugs: 'Got to know the stories if you're going to help people.' Perhaps because I was thinking about The Little House as I watched this scene the connection between stories and help struck home. It felt good to have those Johnny Cash stories in our pub – to have someone singing about what was recognisably our life. Song, music, is of course a more immediately appealing and easy-access medium than serious literature, which often looks, even to practised readers, a bit off-putting. To make a Cash-like connection between the inner and the outer life in the brickmaker's cottage some very powerful writing would be required, and something so pleasurable that it could compete with gin. Who could come up with such stuff? Well Dickens for one. His works were read aloud by the members of communities who could read – in alehouses as well as homes. No one would think of taking Dickens to the illiterate now – the language is too hard, the books are too long, and the modern fear of sentiment too deeply embedded. Yet when I read *A Christmas Carol* aloud in the canteen of Birkenhead YMCA last year, the men around the table, some of them very hard, some of them very bruised, listened with more than interest – they listened like men who were getting hold of something they needed. Sure, the language is hard, the books are long and there are whole swathes where listeners might not understand, but we all feel when the story touches home. It's partly a question also of finding the right book, story or poem for the right reader at the right time. When Cash sang Shel Silverstein's 'A Boy Named Sue' in The Little House we all sang along. We recognised the reality the song pointed to: life is hard and it's going to make *you* hard:

> And he said: 'Son, this world is rough
> And if a man's gonna make it, he's gotta be tough
> And I knew I wouldn't be there to help ya along.
> So I give ya that name and I said goodbye
> I knew you'd have to get tough or die
> And it's the name that helped to make you strong.'

This is the same truth that Christina Rossetti touches on in 'Endure Hardness':

> A cold wind stirs the blackthorn
> To burgeon and to blow,
> Besprinkling half-green hedges
> With flakes and sprays of snow.
>
> Through coldness and through keenness,
> Dear hearts, take comfort so:
> Somewhere or other doubtless
> These make the blackthorn blow.

This is a simple poem but if Alex, our poetry-loving sailor, had recited it we wouldn't have 'got it' despite the fact that it's talking about the same stuff as 'A Boy Named Sue'. For most casual contemporary readers 'Endure Hardness' has problems of language – in the bar of The Little House we wouldn't have known what 'blackthorn' was, wouldn't have had have a clue what 'burgeon' meant, and although some of us might have known that 'blow' was a word for marijuana we'd also know it couldn't mean that here. (The 1968 regulars of The Little House would have been in a state similar to that of contemporary undergraduates, many of whom would have linguistic and cultural problems with the poem.) The thing that might touch a *Reader* magazine reader – the poem's deep meaning – is in the first instance unavailable: the language is too unusual, and the wit and sadness of Rossetti's central word 'doubtless', is thus rendered invisible.

What is lost if readers cannot bridge the gap between an easy-access reading that finds resonance in life (say Johnny Cash lyrics) and the layered complexities of poetry or a narrative like *Bleak House*? If they more or less mean the same why not just enjoy the Cash song? Why bother with what's difficult?

In this issue of *The Reader* we have devoted much of the Learning Curve section to the problems of what or how to teach children to read in schools. At a time when the Poet Laureate is causing upset by suggesting *Paradise Lost* be on every child's reading list while the QCA seems to be suggesting that children need to learn skills for texting, *The Reader* is keen to inspire debate about how to make serious reading a vital part of education.

Of course reading must seem relevant. But relevance may not be so much about subject matter as about personal connection, and that electrical spark can often be provided by a passionate teacher. Above all we need to start with great stories and we need to read them aloud to each other. We need the Dickens touch, so I would offer the equivalent of the Johnny Cash song, because we need to see 'the mud and the blood and the beer' in our stories. Recognition, magic and love have got to come before learning. Once we can trust them, or the voice that is reading, language problems become insignificant. If I could go back in time to my mum's pub, and take just one book, I'd take *The Winter's Tale*. Our customers would know Leontes, kicking off for no good reason, turning on his wife and his best mate, causing his children grief. Leontes might well have 'shot a man in Reno'. And while Shakespeare's vocabulary can be difficult, reading through the strangeness is only a matter of confidence, of practice, which is mostly what – for all the bluster about deconstruction and objective critical skills – educated readers tend to have over uneducated ones. Being adult human beings in the thick of it, whatever their state of education, many of our regulars would already know the deep truth of *The Winter's Tale*'s incredible ending, of Paulina's 'It is required you do awake your faith'. As readers, parents, educators, we must trust difficult books. If we don't believe our children can learn to love them, they won't.

Three Poems by Les Murray

Pastoral Sketches

The sex of a stallion at rest
bulges in subtle fine rehearsal,
and his progeny drop in the grass
like little loose bagpipes.
Wet nap and knotty drones, they lie
glazing, and learning air
then they lever upright, wobbling.
Narrow as two dimensions
they nuzzle their mothers' groin
for the yoghurt that makes girth.

*

The prickly paperbark tree
annually called Snow-in-summer
resembles the fragrant coiffure
of a crowd of senior women;
it joins up into a mountain,
white as Graz, warm as cauliflower.
Pencil holes in the clay soil
are where cicadas woke from their
years of foetus life, to two
two days frantic amethystine.

*

Individuals move round, miles apart,
planning gravel, making access.
Local news is the kind least sold.
Funerals come by radio or phone,
deduction and For Sale bring other bits,
some must even be danced for
at the Hall. *You know Sid's moved? –*
Where to? – Out Gunnedah. –
After only eighty years? – His absence
will be the dark under their house brim.

*

Cleome flowers on improbably lank
spears incline their heads, to fling
free of the booty weight of bees.
Cats freeze and dab, and have to be
screamed back No, Mogg! as a snake
shuffles its suits like a cardsharp's stretch.
Christmas stars detonating violetly
the season comes on with beachwear and bling.
We preferred the no-fly zone of Spring,
and cattle wade in their peaceful tragedy.

The Offshore Island

Terra cotta of old rock undergirds
this mile of haze-green island
whitening odd edges of the sea.

It is unbrowsed by hoofed beasts
and their dung has not been on it.
Trees of the ice age have stayed rare

though no more firesticks come out
from the long smoky continent
lying a canoe-struggle to the west.

The knee-high bush is silvered canes,
bracken, unburnt grasses, bitou.
Miners came, and ate the mutton birds.

Greeks camped there in lean times
fishing. Their Greek islands lived in town
with their families. Now it's National Park.

The world shrinks as it fills.
Outer niches revert to space, in which
to settle is soon too something.

The Weatherproof Jungle Tree

for Margaret Woodward's new hen-house

Pointed at bow and poop
or plumed with flourish astern
chickens crowd out of their coop
with a scratch and a half-turn
into the footwork of forage
unless hailed on by grain,

grain first scattered in the Stone Age
to secure their eggs and meat
by having their cluck around the village,
their filigree down round our feet
and their panic failure of inference
about those we grabbed. So neat.

But everything comes home to roost
now, and points at us with spears;
for our battery Belsens
a virus could be unloosed
at us out of the East
by the mild poultry, it appears –

but it may succumb to research
and if not, horrors pass
and sometime again, fowls will perch
as here, in a weatherproof tree,
a rococo excretory palace
with all its hatching boxes

safe from snakes and from foxes
since, after this red-meat hiatus,
fowls will be back in their billions
because we redesigned their nests,
evolving their breeding, like ours,
up out of the sudden-death grass.

From Anon to Anxiety
The Pleasures and Pains of a Junior Poet

Carol Rumens

Writers often talk about their literary influences as if reading begins with reading. I always think to myself – but what about 'This little Piggie?' or 'Round and Round the Garden?' I suspect those playful, body-based rhymes have more to do with your future work – and certainly with your sense of vocation – than *The Waste Land* or even *The Catcher in the Rye.*

The idea of writing on the body, from the body, does not start with the feminist theorists! Mother and father fingers scribble a tickly circle in our palms, or tweak our toes, and the words sink in through excited nerve-endings even before we learn to speak. We are rocked and jiggled into language, and it will never be so acutely sensed and rhythmically alive again. My parents were both demonstrative and fond of the spin of words, though in quite dissimilar ways, and I, an only child, was their ever-receptive audience.

They both disapproved of 'baby-talk' but they had a compensatory fund of vivid, strange little words and phrases. Ears, for my mother were 'weekies', and for my father, 'lug-holes', which was not quite polite but more fun. My feet were 'tootsies' in my mother's idiolect, and 'plates of meat' in my father's. But no parent had the premium on euphemism or delicacy. The tummy was the 'bellygobuskins' in mother-speak and 'Mary Ann' for my father.

They were both South Londoners, but they had their own distinctive slang. My father's was coloured by the fact that he had been a soldier. But it was an air-force phrase that I heard most often. 'Don't get into a flat spin' he'd say when anyone got in a panic. And when he lifted me on his shoulders it was for a 'flying angel'.

Tongue-twisters were opportunities for my parents to show off their skills, my muddled imitation of 'She sells Sea-Shells' and 'Peter Piper' producing nonsense and giggles – and eventual success. The mnemonics included Days of the Months and weather saws: 'Red sky at night, Shepherd's delight, Red sky in the morning, Shepherd's warning.' Perhaps in suburban Forest Hill we were not so very far from the land. We lived with my maternal grandparents – and in fact both sets of grandparents were originally country people. 'Whistling women and crowing hens / Scare the devils out of the dens' my grandfather would scold darkly when I had learned to whistle. My upbringing was old-fashioned enough for me to have learned the alphabet as a song, just as my grandmother did:

> Sing ABC, DEFG, HIJKLM,
> NOPQ, RSTU, VWXYZ!

It was exciting somehow to expect a full rhyme and get only a distant one.

When at last a poem connected to a book, it was the pictures I read, not the words. It was the counting-rhyme, 'One two, buckle my shoe.' Of course I had heard it chanted, and knew it by heart, but its look on the page was purely pictorial. I remember the short blocks of bold black type, and the shapes of the numbers. The old-fashioned pictures, like fairground mock-porcelain, were the words – or were the words somehow the pictures? I loved the big fat hen and the empty plate, images and words that were completely interchangeable, but I registered the strange verbs like 'delve' and 'a-courting' which the pictures of farmers and milk-maids only half-explained. The textured consonants and strong vowels seemed to draw colours from the gaudy illustrations. A little later, my favourite rhyme was the one about the old woman tossed up in a basket, seventy times as high as the moon. The basket/ask it rhyme delighted me – as did the mixed menace and reassurance of the last line 'But I shall be with you, by and by.'

It was a good time to be growing up with books. By the late nineteen-forties, paper was plentiful again. New books were cheap treats or rewards – symbols of my good behaviour, like tubes of Smarties. I liked it best when I had some idea of what the new book would taste like. Children, like poets, want that special blend of repetition and surprise. That's why series are so popular with children.

I don't remember preferring poems over stories. On the contrary, I have never been so obsessed by a poem as I was by the first story-book I owned. It was called *Dumpy Doodle*. Not a title I expect anyone to recollect. It was an improving threepenny fable about greed.

Dumpy Doodle was an elf addicted to cake. He was always stealing from the other elves. One day they complained to the Fairy Queen. And the next time Dumpy stole cakes, she arranged for them to be turned to stones inside Dumpy Doodle's stomach. Dumpy Doodle cried and cried. There must have been a happy ending tacked on (there always was, in those days) but I don't remember what it was. For me, the story ended with a full-page line-drawing of Dumpy Doodle clutching his stomach and shedding a puddle of tears.

I learned to read with this gruesome parable. I demanded to have it read to me over and over. And when my mother couldn't stand it any more, I pored over the pages by myself, adding memory-sounds and word-shapes. This crudely drawn, cheaply made little Woolworth's book soon succumbed to my four-year-old's literary gluttony, fell to pieces, was glued up, fell apart again and had to be thrown away. I almost forgot about Dumpy Doodle till one day in Woolworth's, fingering my way through the scattering of books on the toy counter, I spotted the exact same scarlet cover. I pleaded urgently and was bought another *Dumpy Doodle*. The same thing happened: the book fell apart and I begged for a new one. It happened every few months, and I don't know how many copies we got through before I finally got thoroughly bored with Dumpy.

I soon learned the concept of 'favourite author' and would grab at any book by Enid Blyton. She was the perfect writer for a small child, didactic and cheerful, and a shade frightening. Perhaps all good authors are parents to their readers, easing our sense of orphanhood, restoring the lost regime in which we once flourished and fretted? Blyton's moral world was cosy and authoritarian and banal. But the aura of safety and reassurance was always cut through by something darker. Her concept of naughtiness verged on evil. She often called her characters 'wicked'. Dispensing scary punishments to these little villains, she was the Mother Grimm of the English suburbs, the nanny of the nanny-less classes. She was like her creation, the Grabbit Chair, whose knobbly wooden arms came to life and embraced any infant wrong-doer and held him down. I felt smug in the chair of the story: of course, I was the good character, but it was thrilling to feel so close to the wicked ones and their punishment.

'The Adventures of Rupert Bear' opened my biggest imaginative world. 'Rupert' was an industry. *The Daily Express* published an episode of his adventures every day. There were cheap monthly paper-cover Ruperts, and a great culmination in the Christmas Annual, whose stories stood up to months – no, years – of re-reading. I first met Rupert through a bunch of old pre-war annuals which had been bought for my aunt Sarah, and I liked those older books particularly. They were printed in dimmer colours than the new annuals, and perhaps that was why the stories seemed more dreamlike.

Over time, the Rupert stories became my vision of the ideal childhood. Rupert led his gang of animal 'pals' on endless mysterious adventures that began in idealised green rolling countryside. He never fought, was never spiteful, and the friends never questioned his benign and reasonable leadership. There were no adult restrictions on their wanderings. Although, in the end, 'the little bear' always returned home safely to his ancient-looking bear parents, he clearly did not have great need of their services.

Arthur Bestall's animals possessed the distinctive features of their species, and had their own witty, peculiarly Victorian, and perhaps rather camp, ways of dressing. Algie Pug wore a bow-tie and a wing collar, like a little canine Etonian, and Pong Ping, the Chinese poodle, sported a black waistcoat and crimson jodhpurs. I think now they were projections of the way children see other children – as vividly unique, as if belonging, each one, to a different species.

It wasn't the psychology or dialogue that mattered: it wasn't even primarily the adventure. It was the curious settings in which the adventures took place, endlessly weird topographies traversed by strange machines. In my favourite, egg-shaped cars ran underground on rails through icy caves and emerged onto the edge of a steep, blueish ice cliff. I longed passionately to be in one of those cars, rushing through a dream-geography encased in perfect safety and suspense.

I read only the rhyming couplets under the pictures, which were four to a page as in a comic. I ignored completely the blocks of explanatory prose underneath. The rhymes were in italics and iambic tetrameter, and galloped along in basic narrative mode. 'Rupert exclaimed: "I'm in the tree!/ Now what does that horse want with me?"' I began to make up narrative couplets too, though my metrical line was rather less regular.

'Sarah's twenty-one, and it won't be long / Before she can work in a rest au rong' I chanted, in response to a great secret my aunt had muttered to me one day when we met unsupervised on the upstairs landing. I remember how her face creased into smiles when I chanted it. How, though she continued to smile, she seemed to become embarrassed, and ducked her head when I sang it in front of Grandma Miles. She was in her late teens at the time. She had Down's Syndrome, but I didn't understand then that her condition meant that her chatter about jobs and future marriage was all fantasy. I think she half sensed it, and that was why my chanting made her shy.

There was a time when life seemed to roll by entirely in couplets. On the bus to Lewisham, where my mother went to the big covered market once a week, there was a conductor with an appropriate rhyme for every fare stage. At Lewisham Hospital he would sing out 'Come along, ladies, mind you don't fall, or you'll end up in the HOS-PI-TALL' and at Eden Park, more cryptically, 'Eden Park, just for a lark!' My mother and I were always happy when he was the conductor on our bus, though he never chatted to us when we laughed and complimented him. I think his head was always busy with the next jingle.

'Come away, oh human child, to the waters and the wild, for the world's too full of weeping for you to understand.' A nun with an Irish accent was reciting to our class, the Upper Kindergarten, aged 6. This was something different: there was a rhyme in it but it didn't fall like a gong on the last word and it didn't make you laugh. At home I sat and wrote a poem about water-fairies, trying to find the same stream-like rhythm for my own words. I can't remember the poem itself, which perhaps suggests it was more complicated than my usual jingles. I remember only that its rhythms and images opened out a real, wild, watery place that I could go to every time I repeated them. It was the first time that I'd connected the sounds and rhythms of verse with emotional intensity and not simply with story-telling. My poem was not just a roll and tumble of words, it was emotional conjury. It opened a different sort of door.

I inherited Sarah's barely-thumbed copy of *A Child's Garden of Verses* but I liked the pictures better than the poems, even though I was a fluent reader by then: I could have stared at them for ever. They looked as if they had been done in the same water-colour paints I was beginning to use – but when this artist dabbed the soft colours over the outlines that were supposed to contain them, it was beautiful and deliberate. It gave you a strange sense of light and shadow and movement and passing summer days.

My attitude to the poems was complicated. It was fine to understand exactly what a poem was about: 'In winter I get up at night/ And dress by yellow candle-light./ In summer quite the other way/I have to go to bed by day/ And hear the grown-up people's feet/ still going past me in the street.' Of course, I had never dressed by yellow candle-light, but I often lay awake in the dim brightness of a summer evening, listening to the noises from outside. I could hear the footsteps when I read Stevenson's line, and when I lay in bed listening to the footsteps I could hear Stevenson's line. At the same time, I felt an odd sense of intrusion. How did he know I felt this? Why was he writing about it and not I? Why was a grown-up pretending to be a child?

My mother couldn't make up stories, and no amount of begging would persuade her to try. I soon accepted that the very word 'story' brought her out in wails. 'My chum and I!' she'd cry, and we'd laugh and remember the terrible occasion when she had begun a school composition with the words 'My chum and I', and the teacher had been so appalled by the word 'chum' that she'd drawn a red line through the whole piece and given my mother nought out of a hundred.

My father, though, was eager to oblige. Once a week, my mother had a night off to go to the flicks with her favourite cousin, Auntie Dora, and this was his opportunity. He didn't tell me a completely new story each week, but invented a weekly 'series', each self-contained episode involving the same set of characters. These tales were not at all like the fairy stories and animal adventures I was used to. My father had found a compromise between the kind of thing he liked writing, I think, and the kind of thing he thought would amuse a child.

It was sit-com, really, set in an English village. There were no children or talking animals, just a few grown-ups who were, without exception, gratifyingly silly. They might have been stereotypes, but to me they were vividly real: the dim Policeman Plod, copied, I would later think, by Enid Blyton in her Mr Plod character in the *Noddy* books, a fussy spinster called Miss Prim, and a hilarious gluttonous vicar who belched in the middle of sermons. My father did the different voices and left plenty of room for audience participation. At the end, the spinster was always outraged, the policeman outwitted and the vicar preached his only sermon:

> Dearly beloved brethren (*belch*) isn't it a sin
> To eat raw potatoes and throw away the skin?
> The skin feeds the pigs (*belch*) the pigs feed us.
> Dearly beloved brethren, what an awful fuss! (*BELCH*).

My father and I chanted this together, always punctuating the sermon with the most revolting burps we could devise.

After I'd gone to sleep, he then sat down at the dining-table to write his own story or poem.

By the time my mother came home spinning on her high heels in imitation of Ginger Rogers or humming the 'Harry Lime' theme my father would usually have completed something. If he'd finished a story, and was happy with it, he would offer to read it to my mother. But if it was a poem he'd written, he simply tucked it in a drawer. He knew my mother hated that depressing sob-stuff, poetry.

'I told him to send them to the papers, but he never did. He didn't keep them. No. They disappeared. No idea what happened to them.' So my mother said, and I believe her: my father was a painfully modest man. He never showed me a single thing he wrote. Though he treated my little poems and stories kindly, it was as if he did not want to acknowledge any connection between my writerly ambition and his.

Early in January 2000, I made a pilgrimage. I went to the City of London, and found, in the shadow of Lloyd's totem-pole tower, and not far from the cracked humpty-dumpty of the 'gherkin', the short, twisty corridor of a road called Billeter Street. Here, I knew, was the site of Dock House, a grand Venetian-style building where my father had worked as a young shipping clerk. It had been bombed in the Blitz of 1941. I worked out its position by the numbering, and by the fact that the replacement building had in its stone porch a small carved anchor, which was the Dock House symbol. It seemed to suggest commemoration..

The new building turned out to be empty. There was nothing, no plate or plaque, to show its ownership. The company that owned it, like my father's company, must have gone bust.

I looked through a dusty window at workmen's ladders and bits of masonry: another renovation. The existence of a basement gym was advertised on the door: it wasn't open, though the sign looked fresh. There was no-one about.

My father's century had finished. He had died in 1979. He wasn't going to come even a little way into the twenty-first with my mother and me. I left my spray of freesias on the pavement outside the hollow building, pausing to imagine his daily footsteps there.

That night I dreamt I had somehow got into the gym. I passed rows of exercise machines, and went into a tiny back room. It was lined with shelves, tiny ones, like those designed for CDs. In each small compartment were crammed the paintings and drawings, the stories and poems, I'd produced as a child.

He had smuggled them into work and hidden them there. He had filled the dark pleats of the shelves with these brightly crayoned and painted little artefacts so as to keep them safe, and to show me that I was special to him. Perhaps I had entered his mind, and these were his memories?

He didn't like anything I wrote when I was older. He hated 'modern poetry' and by the time my first book was published he had dementia and was no longer able to read, let alone write. He only loved my child-poet self, which he hoped would never change.

I didn't grow up completely innocent of TV. Like so many other families, my grandparents bought their first set early in 1953, so they could watch Elizabeth the Second's Coronation.

We were invited to inspect the new wonder. Grandpa Miles, flushed with pride, turned the switch and the mudgreen window bloomed slowly into a flickering greyish line of chorus-girls in big flouncy skirts, sedately kicking their legs to exactly the same height, predetermined so you couldn't see their knickers, I surmised, only the tops of their stockings. My father wolf-whistled rudely. 'OOOOH' Sarah said, a rare light coming into her eyes. 'I could kick like that once' cried my mother, hauling her skirt up slightly to demonstrate that she still almost could. I didn't catch my breath: it was only like the films, after all. But later, when there was something called 'commercial television', which meant ads, I was hooked.

'Dirty again, dirty again, oh my, dirty again' I sang, racing round our tiny living room in imitation of the little cartoon housewife who darted about her little house whisking off tablecloths and picking up scattered clothes for salvation by Persil.

Then it was:

> You'll wonder where the yellow went
> When you go steady with Pepsodent.

Or

> Murray Mints, Murray Mints,
> Too-good-to-hurry mints!

So, at the age of eight or nine, I tuned in to the modern nursery rhymes, TV jingles – a little late, probably, for them to imprint my deeper brain, yet no more possible to forget than 'One, two, buckle my shoe.'

The Coronation went on for ever, delighting my mother and Grandma May, boring Sarah and me. At school, our class had been painting orbs and sceptres, coaches and thrones, for weeks, using up masses of chrome yellow powder paint. And now here they were, grey and disappointing – orb, sceptre, coach, throne, the Queen herself – a small pale anxious pixy-face at the top of a heap of luxurious clothes.

My mother began making a Coronation scrapbook, with pictures cut out of the magazines and Special Supplements, and a red-white-blue striped satin ribbon as bookmark. 'We are the best country in the world,' she told me. 'We are only very small but we are great.' I knew we had won the war, so I supposed she was right.

The first lines of Shakespeare I ever heard were during the Coronation: 'This royal throne of kings, this sceptred isle… This precious stone set in the silver sea' said a hushed, resonant male voice-over that suddenly made my spine tingle. It was not because I was proud of the great little island, but because of the magic way a dull invisible thing, a country, had been turned into a gemstone, and how it shone in Shakespeare's words, small and perfect and emerald, with a fence of golden sceptres holding it in place in its silver setting. Perhaps it was my first experience of a metaphor. And yet my admiration was tinged by a new, sour sensation. It was jealousy. Why couldn't I write a 'poem' as good as that?

And so that first innocence of the adoring reader was lost. I became a little would-be writer, worrying whether I could ever be as good as Shakespeare. And though the answer to that one soon became cruelly clear, the 'anxiety of influence' never quite went away. I still constantly fall in love with books. But I don't think the question of comparison is ever entirely banished from my mind. Could I do that, if only I could do that, haven't I done something almost as good as that – what sad little egotistical mutterings. Only Anon is completely lovable, untaintable. Sometimes I wish all literature was 'by' Anon.

> And seeing the snail, which everywhere doth roam,
> Carrying his own house still, still is at home,
> Follow (for he is easy paced) this snail,
> Be thine own palace, or the world's thy gaol.
>
> John Donne, 'To Sir Henry Wotton'

Two Poems by Caroline Price

Two Pieces from Josefov

i. Synagogue

After the roll-call written in red and black
across every wall –
after the thousands of names printed
shoulder to shoulder
covering every inch, each curve
in the stone, each seam and corner –
after walking past row on row
of 80,000, delicate red black red
like the grain in brick, the names
of the dead of Bohemia and Moravia

to escape into this, the hilly relief
of green and grey,
tombs sprouting in picturesque clumps
from the crowded ground
like families gathered, generations thrust close
by hands from below;
so plain medieval sandstone
is propped against later carved marble, cut
to show status or trade: here for example
the scissors of a tailor.

ii. Golem

They stream, the rucksacked teenagers,
past pictures, names

and out into the cemetery, a rush of colour
along its paths. Talismans

hang from their straps. They know
about the *formless thing*, protector of the ghetto

created from the elements, brought to life
four centuries ago

by Rabbi Löw; they know the custom
of heaping small, respectful pebbles

on his tomb. And crowd round, scribbling
on hand-shaded scraps

which they fold and press like pellets of gum
into all the cracks and crevices

of his monument – whatever they have written
after coming out of darkness

into the light; whatever messages they have,
whatever they hope to conjure

from what surrounds them, water, earth, air.

Conversation over Dessert

Jane Davis talks with Len Rodberg, one-time advisor to the Kennedy administration, near-miss rabbi, scientist and activist about the books that have changed his life

Len Rodberg

Can you remember learning to read?
No. The first memory I have of reading is when I was nine years old. Although I did well in school I don't have any memory of what I was reading or what my mother was reading to me. I only remember what I read when I was nine years old which is what I view as the first real book I read.

What was that?
The book was… OK, I'll step back a bit, I woke up to the world on December 7th 1941 when I was just about nine years old.

What happened then that woke you up?
Pearl Harbor. I remember sitting in front of the radio listening to Roosevelt giving his speech to Congress. So, my memory of involvement with the world, with the outer world, and with reading is shaped by WW2. I mean obviously I must have read children's books but what I remember reading is *Guadalcanal Diary* written by Richard Tregaskis. It's the story of the invasion of Guadalcanal by the US Marines which took place some time in March or April 1942.

How did you come across such a book?
My parents bought it for me. I also read Ernie Pyle. Ernie Pyle was a reporter who wrote a diary detailing the experiences of real-life GIs, real-life soldiers. I remember reading that and a couple of military biographies. And then I read *Newsweek* magazine, my father subscribed to *Newsweek* magazine. As far as I know that was the only thing he read apart from the newspapers. He didn't read books. It came once a week and it told the progress of the war.

What did your father do for a living?
He was a candy salesman, a travelling salesman. He represented Blumenthal Brothers Candy. Starting with the invasion of Normandy, which was two years later in 1944, I did a personal clipping service. I kept what I called a war diary, which had clippings from each day, and I was making a book. Each page represented where the war stood that day.

Were you frightened by the war or were you just interested in it?
No, I wasn't frightened. It was an adventure and I had a telescope and I would sit out in a tree in my back yard as a civilian spotter! I was waiting for the German aeroplanes to come over. We had these silhouettes posted in the tree of what they looked like, so I would know one if I saw it. My parents also bought me *The Book of Knowledge*, a twenty-volume encyclopaedia for children. I was probably twelve or thirteen then and I read it, all of it, from cover to cover.

Were you beginning to know that you would be a scientist by then?
No, not until two things had happened. One was the explosion of the atomic bomb in 1945. I was at junior high school, ninth or tenth grade, so I was thirteen years old.

Did that seem like a triumph?
No, it seemed like an interesting scientific development that would affect the world. I didn't see the tragic aspect of it… just the amazement.

Almost excitement?
Yes, that science could do this. If I continue chronologically, I had a teacher as a senior – this just shows we are all people of many parts – who was a really funny old man. He seemed like a classic figure, he was thin with a pince-nez (this was 1950) and he taught me *Hamlet*. It was also the same year, I think, that Olivier's film came out and I was blown away. I mean we'd read *Julius Caesar* and we'd read *Romeo and Juliet* and *Macbeth*, but none of them did anything for me. But *Hamlet*, with this guy who really loved it, who was such a charismatic, strange figure, that did something for me. I don't know what because I didn't become an English person. In college I skipped all the standard literary courses and took a world literature course, so I did that part, and at least I got that.

What books changed your life?
That's an interesting thing to consider. I was going to be a rabbi for

a little while, when I was eighteen.

You said before we began the interview that wanting to be a rabbi was related to wanting to 'repair the world'. Do you think there's a connection between that and the excitement of the atomic bomb? Is there an underlying connection?
No, my political development came much later. I didn't get really seriously political until 1960. I was still a technophile in the 1950s and was really interested in inter-continental missiles and all the fabulous technology in development then. But there was one book, *Judaism and Modern Man: An Interpretation of Jewish Religion* by Will Herberg, which clarified for me what I felt about Judaism. It was a existentialist perspective on Judaism as a culture. It allowed me to feel that Judaism was important to me as a source of values and a world view without having to believe in a God who acted in people's lives.

Did your parents believe in God?
I don't think so.

And did you have a Bar Mitzvah?
Yes, they did the formal thing but they never talked about God or religion. I was a scientist and I came back from college one year and we had a college student night and I gave a sermon entitled 'God and the Electron'. My understanding of belief in God was the regularity of natural law. And Herberg was one book that really put it together for me which I read sometime at the end of high school and the beginning of college.

Was it the Will Herberg book that prompted you to want to become a rabbi?
No, that came later. I was interested in Judaism but my ideas were still confused. I looked up to the rabbi I had; he was someone I could talk to and his world view seemed to make sense to me. It seemed a good role to play and I was very interested in Judaism as a subject, as a philosophy.

That's interesting considering that your parents weren't practising Jews.
They weren't intellectuals so they didn't really talk about these things. I was brought up with Reform Judaism. So basically the prophets Amos and Hosea, the prophets of justice, they made a big impact on me, still do. Then I went to graduate school and I got involved in the movement of scientists to control nuclear energy.

How did you go from being a technophile to this?

I was starting to make some connections. I was a graduate student, so I was doing physics *and* I was active in the synagogue, various synagogues, on what was called the Social Action Committee. This held discussions and tried to get the synagogues to be active in current social issues. This was a period of McCarthyism so the issue of arms control did not become a public one until the late 1950s and then I got involved in it. Very quickly I got on the board of the Federation of American Scientists. It still exists, and it advocates the control of nuclear energy amongst other things. Then Kennedy was elected and one of his policies was the creation of a disarmament agency so I joined his administration by applying for a job as their scientist – they were looking for a scientist. It all fit together. Then I read a book written by a colleague who had joined the same day, Richard Barnett, who became a very well-known writer on foreign policy. He had written a book called *Who Wants Disarmament?* which was a seminal book for me. However, I'm not sure if the book changed me or if I was just ready for the message the book delivered to me. Barnett's message was that it was not the Soviet Union that stands in the way of us getting disarmament; it's both the Soviet Union and the United States. So partly it was the attitude of the United States wanting to be hegemonic in the world. Plus his analysis of the Russians was interesting because I didn't know anything about Russia. I mean I'd read Russian foreign policy but I didn't know anything about Russia itself. What I understood because of Barnett was the defensiveness of the Russians and the experiences the Russians had had of being overrun by the West, repeatedly. What I learned was to look at other countries' foreign policy and behaviour from the point of view of *those* countries and try to understand what they were seeing and not just think of it from an American point of view. So even though it was a short, simple popular text written in 1959 or 1960, it was very important for me. It prompted me to do a lot more reading on the subject.

You read this after you joined the administration?

Yes. I joined the administration because I was concerned about the rational use of nuclear energy and wanted to work on getting a nuclear test ban as a first step. Another seminal book for me, which I later quoted to a lot of people, was *The Coming of the Golden Age: A View of the End of Progress* by Gunther Stent, which I read in the late 1960s. It argued that most of the sciences are complete, for example, the fundamental laws of chemistry and physics are understood and also biology. Only the field of neuroscience and the brain remained at that time where such laws were not really understood.This was the 1960s. The point of this for me was that I was in the process of leaving physics for politics. I didn't teach physics, mostly I taught the social impact of science. However, this book provided me with a reason to leave physics because physics was a mature science which could not contribute any more. One of the reasons I became a physicist after the nuclear bomb was because it seemed to be a field where you could really contribute. However, it became clear to me in the course of the 1960s that nothing new was happening.

You say there is no connection between that little boy watching the bomb and the rabbi's need to repair the world but here you are talking again about your need to contribute and help. There is a connection.
Well, it wasn't clear to me then, it matured over time.

Isn't that interesting? If this were a novel, we would make so much of that little boy in 1945 seeing that explosion.
I hardly ever read fiction. Finally when I was seventeen I read *The Adventures of Tom Sawyer*. And the same summer I read *The Fountainhead*, it took me the whole summer.

I don't know it.
It's Ayn Rand's book about who I was. Her most famous book was *Atlas Shrugged* which is about an architect, a Frank Lloyd Wright character, who is this eccentric who designs buildings and he designs this building for a corporation which is full of character. But the corporation decides that his design is too radical so they fancy it up and he gets furious and blows it up. I loved that – standing up for principle in the most extreme way!

You were how old then?
Seventeen.

These connections between the novel and your life, which a reader would have noticed although you initially didn't, were ultimately discovered by you in the act of reading – is that right? The books being the connection, act as the catalyst…
Yes, the books didn't necessarily create the idea but they put together things that were already circulating in my head. What *The End of Science* did was allow me to leave physics and to go full time into the politics I had been doing whilst in the government. This book made me realise that I wasn't leaving something socially useful for something that wasn't, I was doing the reverse. The book was confirming.

Given that your political career must have been mainly discouraging, were there any books that kept your spirits up? Being as left-wing as you are in America is pretty hopeless really!
Das Kapital. I read it in the early 1970s. I was at this left-wing institute, which was liberal but it wasn't Marxist, and a group of us wanted to look at economics. I was introduced to this book and I started to read it and I realised it was like a physics book. It had a set of hypotheses in the first chapter of how the economy works and then it all fit together and it all made sense to me and it allowed me to understand how the economy works even though it's become much more consumerist. The core structures are still there even though the working class is not what it used to be.

Are you still a Marxist?
Yes.

There are not many left now!
Well the problem is what do you mean by 'Marxist'? I say I am but people say I shouldn't because most people don't understand what Marxist means. It's been so corrupted by the Soviet Union and lots of other things, but as an analytical framework for understanding the structure of the world and the economy we live in, I find it very helpful. It still works for me. And there are additions to it, for example, there is an article by Eric Olin Wright, which lays out the class structure of modern capitalism in the only way that I've ever seen that really works. It was eye-opening for me. For example, what do you do with the middle class? From Marx's perspective there is no middle class. Wright provides answers to these problems.

Marxist theory is another framework, like physics, which you use to try and explain reality and fix it.
Yes, aren't we all looking for explanations? Many people want to know the meaning of life, I don't because I don't believe there is a meaning to life but there is organisation to the physical world and to the world we've created. And it's important to understand and put it in a context where you can try and make some changes.

The place where you work now is multidisciplinary. Is there a good multidisciplinary book that would be useful to people?
No, I keep saying that I'm *non*disciplinary. But there is a seminal book by Peter Manicas. He used to teach at Queens College where I am now, and he wrote a book called *History and Philosophy of the Social Sciences*. What was eye-opening and very clarifying for me as

I moved from physicist to political economist was that it described the history and origins of the social sciences in Germany in the late 1800s when these artificial divisions were established between sociology and psychology and philosophy. The discovery that these divisions were artificial allowed me to ignore them and examine how things really worked. I write a lot of things these days around health care reform and the economics of the American healthcare system and I feel fine writing about it, even though I don't have a PhD in economics.

You still know what you want to say?
Yes, you can still know what you want to say and understand that those distinctions are arbitrary and artificial.

Four Poems by Julie-ann Rowell

The 'It Don't Matter' Café

I was sitting in the 'It Don't Matter' Café
at the window by the silver buttonwood tree,
when a man called Joshua, jammed in the seat behind,
said *God will judge each and every one of us*
by our own pride. Couldn't hear his friend's reply.

I waited on my double espresso from the waitress
whose smile spelt bona fide. Could've kissed her hand,
and waved to the passers-by, in that kind of a mood
for double or nothing, scribbling in my notebook
like someone who had important things to say.

Joshua was searching for spiritual enlightenment.
I couldn't see his face but I liked his voice's cadence,
slicing clear through the fug of the yellow room,
passing on the word of a God I don't believe in
but I could've hugged Joshua without call for reason.

A Walk at Coney Island

We ate genuine Nathan hotdogs on the snow-crushed beach,
the Russians were coming, crunching along the boardwalk
arm-in-arm, heavy in their furs. Someone had capped
a snowman with a Belisha beacon. You took my photograph.
The sun was all glare and I said it would come out dark.
And the freak shows were closed and the skeletal fairground
creaked in the wind and you held my hand to keep me upright
because it was then I felt consumed by life finding out how
to practise marking time. The last winter, ever. Ever glowing
snow and stunning icicles. Your cold kiss like dynamite.

Skaters at Lake Michigan

The last time I saw snow and ice like this
it was bunched high in Devon hedgerows;
we were still a family recognised as brothers
and sisters together. We had chilblains then
but thought nothing of it. Watching skaters
as they turn and balance and spin
the air feels blue in my stunned lungs,
even the miracle of ten-inch icicles
passes me by in the wind chill factor minus
something unaccountable. The urge
is to hurry though the legs won't oblige.
It hurts to be outside.

Chicago, March 2003

The snow has dwindled to a black slug
rimming the sidewalks. Icicles are trying to kill us
from ledges of skyscrapers no one can see.

English winters don't take so long to die,
don't tease with violence. We don't have signs
warning of dangers from on high.

How we relish our tall vanilla lattes; for once
more is good. The window shows Lake Michigan
breaking its frozen nose on the foreshore.

Tolstoy
On Life's Verge

Josie Billington

In the penultimate book of *Anna Karenina*, Anna commits suicide, propelled by the increasing incoherence and unreality of her life as wife (of Karenin) *and* mistress (of Vronsky), as mother of Serezha (Karenin's son, whom she loves) *and* of little Anna (Vronsky's daughter, whom she doesn't):

> Well, I get divorced and become Vronsky's wife! What then? … Will Serezha stop asking and wondering about my two husbands? … I thought I loved him, too … yet I lived without him and exchanged his love for another's … I cannot imagine a situation in which life would not be a torment … But when you see the truth, what are you to do?

In Book Eight, the last of the novel, Constantine Levin's contrastingly normal adult life points, almost madly, to the same conclusion:

> 'Without knowing what I am, and why I am here, it is impossible to live. Yet I cannot know that and therefore I can't live.' … And though he was a happy and healthy family man, Levin was several times so near to suicide that he hid a cord lest he should hang himself, and he feared to carry a gun lest he should shoot himself.

Levin is saved, in all senses, when a chance remark from a peasant worker recalls him to the literal meaning of a Christian life:

> 'To live not for one's needs but for God! For what God! What could be more senseless than what he said? … Well? And did I not understand those senseless words of Theodore's? And having understood them, did I doubt their justice? Did I find them stupid, vague or inexact?
>
> 'No, I understand him just as he understands them: understood completely and more clearly than I understand anything in life; and I have never in my life doubted it, and cannot doubt it … at the first hint I understand him! … It is exactly *this* that I know and that we all know.'

The mystery of Levin's revelation is that it is no mystery at all. 'What gladdens me? What have I discovered?' Levin asks himself. 'I have discovered nothing. I have only perceived what it is that I know.' Time and again in Tolstoy's work, belief is a happening of mental catch-up – like the instantaneous correction of some neurological misfire or mistime – where, 'at the first hint', the obvious becomes suddenly *obvious*, as if for the first time, why not to commit suicide.

Virginia Woolf famously described George Eliot's *Middlemarch* as 'one of the few English novels written for grown-up people'. *Anna Karenina* is a novel written for people who have done all that qualifies them to be grown-up, yet who feel anything but complete. Book Eight seems to offer an anticipatory answer to Tom Brangwen's question in D. H. Lawrence's *The Rainbow* – a man, like Levin, faltering in mid-life: 'When did one come to an end? In which direction was it finished? ... There was no peace, however old one grew!' And perhaps the point is that *Anna Karenina* is *not* an English novel. It is a matter of record that the speed of modernisation in Russia in the nineteenth century not only was *too* accelerated to disengage the ancient models of religious belief, but also helped to revive them. In one of those new-old religions, Tolstoyism, the indefatigable truth-seeker in Tolstoy lived out the implications of Levin's revelation, to the scorn of his literary admirers, Lawrence among them: 'Better Anna Karenina, passion and death than Tolstoi and Tolstoi-ism and that beastly peasant blouse the old man wore'. The realist novel in England was concerned with difficulties similar to those that troubled Anna and Levin, but it was life-immersed and this-worldly as it asked on behalf of its increasingly secularised readership the terrible, ordinary questions: What is my life? What am I? Only the Tolstoyan realist novel held out the possibility of a religious solution to those questions in a secular world. To wish away the religious seeker in Tolstoy is to wish away those moments where even the non-believing reader can believe *in* believing, even while asking, with Levin, Can *this* be belief? 'Can I possibly have found the solution of everything?'

The power to transmit the thrill of belief is something generic to Tolstoyan realism. The reality Tolstoy writes of seems to originate with him. 'One reads with such curiosity and naïve astonishment,' says Chekhov of *War and Peace*, 'as though one had never read anything before.' 'He instinctively refused to see people and things in terms of others before him' (from Henri Troyat, Tolstoy's biographer). 'He looked at the world with the eyes of a man who has read nothing and learned nothing, who is discovering everything for himself.'

Struck by the contrast between the incomparable imaginative breadth of the novels and the unfairly self-willed and self-preoccupied man he finds in Tolstoy's letters, Dan Jacobson, in *Adult Pleasures*, concludes that the author starts from his incapacity *as a man* ever to get outside a single first-person view:

> One insistently feels [there] to be a connection between Tolstoy's capacity to be wholly himself, even remorselessly himself … and the capacity of the novelist to fill the consciousness of his characters with a sense of their own autonomy and significance.

Paradoxically, Tolstoy's solipsistic refusal ever to know or to be something in his novels that he could not be in life helps to make a discovery like Levin's *not* his alone but one available to be shared by writer, protagonist and reader all at once. Egoistically generous, Tolstoy's work has that power 'to unite people in the same feelings' which made all true art religious for Tolstoy – not play or pleasure, as he insists in *What is Art?* – but 'a means of human communication, necessary for life'.

'What is the connexion of that man with my childhood and my life?' Prince Andrew of *War and Peace* asks himself when, after his fatal wounding in the battle of Borodino, he sees at the ambulance station the man (Kuragin) who has rivalled his love for Natasha and prevented his marriage to her:

> And suddenly a new unexpected memory … presented itself to him. He remembered Natasha as he had seen her for the first time at the ball of 1810 … and love and tenderness for her, stronger and more vivid than ever, awoke in his soul. He now remembered the connexion that existed between himself and this man … He remembered everything … and wept tender loving tears for his fellow men, for himself, and for his own and their errors.

Prince Andrew's tears are the result of a deeply, yet surprisingly, familiar recognition that between the rival and himself the likenesses are greater than the differences. At this moment of revelatory memory of his essential 'connexion' to Natasha, to Kuragin and to every human creature, Prince Andrew simply forgets who he now is: disillusioned soldier, cynical government official, rejected lover. As though it were a kind of death, the experience destroys the self as such. But something of this kind of involuntary recognition – 'It is exactly *this* I know', as Levin said – is one with which every reader of Tolstoy will be familiar, and even take for granted, without a thought for its 'religious' significance. For Tolstoy it was the surest sign of true art: 'Usually, when a person receives a truly artistic impression,' he says in *What is Art?*, 'it seems to him that he knew it all along, only he was unable to express it … it seems to him that the perceived object has been made, not by someone else, but by himself.' Tolstoyan truth is something fully alive, an idea re-*presented*, made as fleshly as oneself, made, while it lives, one's own! – even in thereby cancelling a sense of oneself as simply separate. Yet for that very reason, Tolstoyan truth, artistic or religious (Tolstoy barely knew a difference), *can* only live in its own unfolding. Tolstoy – like Shakespeare – was as unparaphraseable as he was original. 'If I were to try to say in words,' Tolstoy wrote of *Anna Karenina*, 'everything that I intended to express in my novel, I would have to write the same novel I wrote from the beginning.'

Levin's religious experience is analogously untranslatable. Reproving his coachman immediately after his moment of vision, Levin finds he is as obstinately untransformed as the life which carries on beyond the moment:

> Just as it always did, interference vexed him, and he immediately felt how wrong had been his conclusion that his spiritual condition could at once alter his manner when confronted with reality.

The troubling and authenticating aspect of Levin's revelation is that it does not last and does not change anything much. Likewise, it is only at the point of near-death that Prince Andrew can achieve the new relation to his world and to others which Levin has earnestly looked for. If only it were not 'too late' Prince Andrew thinks, but even were he able to return to life, he would be no better than he is earlier in the novel. He listens to Pierre Bezukhov's enthusiastic rapture over the teaching of the Masonic Brotherhood,

> and something that had long been slumbering, something that was best within him, suddenly awoke, joyful and youthful, in his soul. It vanished as soon as he returned to the customary conditions of life, but he knew that this feeling that he did not know how to develop existed within him.

The problem is that what is 'best' in Prince Andrew, that which he most really is and even knows himself to be, is that which he least knows how to translate into the narrow reality of mortal life. His real self slumbers or is forgotten within the context of ordinary existence as involuntarily as it was remembered in the extraordinary conditions of approaching death. And this was the lifetime baffling paradox for Tolstoy: if there is something inside human beings more real than anything else which even so cannot be realised within the limits of a human life, then how real or properly settled can this human life finally be? One could not carry over those truths into life's continuity. One could only begin again 'from the beginning'. This is why Tolstoy writes like a man who has never *written* anything before, bringing back the same questions again and again in his protagonists, needing these truths repeated explicitly in each character, brought back to life in the right form, at the right time, in order really to know them or even to deserve to know them again.

Dan Jacobson writes:

> I can remember vividly the naïve disappointment I felt at the end of *War and Peace* – which had gripped me so intensely that, like a child, I had positively begrudged the time spent away from it – when I realised that the book had taken up my life for weeks on end without actually making it any easier for me to manage the rest of my life, now that I was to be left on my own once more.

Perhaps this naïve disappointment in the aftermath of reading Tolstoy is the necessary corollary of Chekhov's naïve enthusiasm in the midst of it, just as the loss of certainty suffered by the Tolstoyan protagonist seems to be the price paid for vivid conviction. More usually, as was the case with Lawrence, it is the stubborn presence in the novels of the need for certainty which is regretted by readers. As early as *The Cossacks*, Turgenev was complaining of 'that tedious unhealthy figure, always preoccupied with himself'. 'Why does Tolstoy not rid himself of that nightmare?'

Yet Tolstoy's needs and struggles and, above all, his mistakes were what triggered the novelist in Tolstoy. Indeed it is as if the great Tolstoyan novel, its wonderfully abundant life, is what happened when Tolstoy let the relativising form of the novel turn his mistakenly fierce absolutism into a virtue. That sounds quite complicated. I'll rephrase it and give an example. The multiplicity of absolutes in and across his books makes a rich relativism that helps to atone for all that life cannot resolve. Thus Prince Andrew, when first he hears Natasha sing, finds himself overcome by

> A sudden, vivid sense of the terrible contrast between something infinitely great and illimitable within him, and that limited and material something that he, and even she, was.

'And even she…' Life's relativism teaches that there is nothing on earth commensurate with the immensity of the need he experiences, even as the material creature before him has helped to activate the illimitable need from within his own limited flesh-and-blood self. Novelistic relativism, on the other hand, allows that what remains a problem for Prince Andrew here might offer an alternative and better solution to Anna's situation than Anna's own, where death seems to replace life as casually as Vronsky replaced Serezha. The thought that she might have been saved by the recognition that no *person* could ever be the answer to her repeated question 'What do I want?' does not save her, of course, but it helps to save the memory and meaning of her. It helps us to know who Anna *was* that in doubt of her own ability to love she continually sought her answers in the fallible people around her until she could seek no longer. The chance of salvation by another approach does not occur to her.

To read the Tolstoyan novel is to discover that apparently opposite things – 'suffering and freedom', war and peace, Anna and Levin, or Anna and Prince Andrew – while the contrasts are illuminating and meaningful, are not as simply opposed as they might seem but 'very near together'. Yet Tolstoy himself could take no comfort from this novelistic connection-making: to do so would have seemed like a form of cheating. He was strongly aware that while a person could be many different things, (innocently enough) she or he could only be *one* thing at any *one* time. Again and again we come back to that obstinacy of untranslatable feeling. That same distinctive phenomenon – the capacity for one being to incorporate opposing modes of existence and expression which are equally autonomous and which therefore cannot be incorporated into one another – is what enables Prince Andrew abruptly to *forgive* Kuragin and also, so the novel discloses, what enables Natasha to *forget* Prince Andrew. 'Three days?' says Natasha when she meets Kuragin, soon after her betrothal to Prince Andrew. 'It seems to me I've loved him a hundred years. It seems to me that I have never loved anyone before.' How potent and selfish and complete, and how fringed by an unfelt lament those words are.

The more you delve into the soul, the mind, the character of a person, wrote Tolstoy, late in life, 'the more one finds what is common and familiar to all'. The slightest hint could turn Anna into Levin, or Prince Andrew into Natasha. What the later, sparer, more austere Tolstoyan works do is to distil these recognitions and make religious use of their implications – as if writing were always, for Tolstoy, a way of putting wrong or troubling life-matters into places where they could *become* right or at least clear. Natasha and Prince Andrew, for instance, are only as different from one another as Vasily Andreevich is different from himself when in the Christian parable, *Master and Man*, he first leaves his peasant worker to die in a snowstorm in a desperate attempt to save himself, and then, having literally gone round in circles in his effort to find the road, comes back to the same spot where Nikita is freezing to death:

> Vasily Andreevich stood silent and motionless for half a minute. Then suddenly, with the same resolution with which he used to shake hands when making a good purchase, he took a step back and began raking the snow off Nikita ... covering him not only with his fur coat but with the whole of his body ...
>
> 'There, and you say you're dying. Lie still and get warm, that's our way ...' began Vasily Andreevich.
>
> But to his great surprise he could say no more ... He stopped speaking and only gulped down the risings in his throat. 'Seems I was badly frightened and have gone quite weak,' he thought. But his weakness was not only not unpleasant, but gave him a peculiar joy such as he had never felt before.

Vasily Andreevich's greatest deed is no more than a redirection of the 'same resolution' which has produced his most fallen deeds. From damnation to salvation – or back again – at just one step. No wonder Tolstoy turned his back upon the largeness, and looseness, of the novels. For it was only by strictly narrowing himself to a single protagonist's field of vision that he could prevent himself from being distracted by his own gift for life and make possible the continual, if precarious embodiment of a better self. There is nothing dull or formulaic about the incarnation of religious principle here. The unamended word 'weakness' shows how unprecedented the 'peculiar joy' is. If prizing this magnificent, tireless innocence seems like valuing the man more than the work (reversing Lawrence's dictum 'his books were better than his life') then so be it. Tolstoy himself made no distinction. 'You think that I am one thing and my writing is another,' he wrote to his wife. 'But my writing is the whole of me ... All my works ... have been nothing more or less than my life.' The books mattered as the outcome of a life, and a search for meaning within it, which was incontestably greater than the books ever could be in themselves. Art for life's sake, to its very verge.

Two Poems by Roz Goddard

Lenin, 1923

Lenin has come to this: a bathchair
among brambles, two carers fighting
nature with sticks. They have pushed him
to the ground's forgotten edge, imagining
in these last days, he might glimpse fairies.

Convinced that fresh air is healing they rumble
on, muttering to each other that he might
be better hitching a piggy back. A stone intervenes
stops that foolish thought before it elicits a wince
from the great man.

Lenin longs to rise, race over the unevenness
of fields, feel the unmistakable crush of fungus
on his soles. He stares ahead, his chair possessed
as midges dance a complex semaphor
inches from his face.

My Niece's Head

Her eyes are brimming blue
leaking their own colour
traces of salt across pale cheeks
impossible for her mother to kiss away
those days are ancient history.

Her lip is swollen to a slug, blood easing
down her perfect chin. She looks at the carpet.
Her face all movement, seismic shifts
beneath her skin. Glass becomes liquid again.

She's a child with the look of an abandoned woman
nose running from another long night waiting.
Yet, I'm detecting in her something of the earth:
birds, grass on the motorway verge, a song…

Beautiful Lands

Sasha Dugdale

I suppose you might call it a brutal coming-of-age. Yes, a coming of age, although in fact I felt younger, a child, bewildered beyond words after it all happened. I looked for ways to send it out of my mind. It came to me that the whole incident was a dream, and it is true that the shame and the horror are vague and shifting, as if I had felt them in a dream. But it also came to me afterwards, much later, that we are the world's children, cosseted to the end, and the rest of the world looks over us in our lifelong innocence. Is it our fault? I am never awake, but I am turning my life over and over in my mind and wondering at it. I am wiser now, I have seen more, but I cannot forget my sense of shame.

I had finished school. Our school days were over at last and by the summer most of my friends had fanned out across the continents, taking boots and backpacks, old clothes and traveller's cheques. I worked for some months in a shop to earn the money to travel and I used to bring my post from around the world to work and sit up in the staffroom at break time studying the letters and photographs, reading the captions: This is me. This is the desert road. And here I am with the kids I teach. Briefly I was left behind, aching to be off and away, as I imagined it, with the desert road behind me and the sun in my hair.

In late autumn it was my turn to leave. I took a local train from the town to the airport. An old lady got on with me, she had known me since I was small and she asked where I was going. I tell her. You lucky girl, she said. Send me a postcard, although I expect you'll be too busy for that. I promised I would send her a card and I wrote her address in my notebook. This is where I am going to write down all my experiences, I told her. Oh my, she said. You'll have to get that published when you get back. She was perched on the seat, bird-like in her skirt and coat. She had an amber brooch on her collar and she was going, she said, to see her friend for lunch. My backpack was unwieldy and seemed to cover most of the bank of seats. I had put my oldest teddy in at the top and to my embarrassment his ratty ears were poking out.

This is the last conversation I had until I arrived. I was too stiff with my own pride and my need to be self-sufficient to chat on the plane, or even in the hostel. There was a day or two hanging around in the wet falling snow collecting tickets and provisions. I was a loner during this time – demonstratively so. And then it was the evening and I made my way to the station like a snail under my heavy bag. I bought a few last bits in a small glass kiosk – and as I turned towards the platform I caught sight of myself in a sheet of mirroring glass on a shop front. I looked different. Yes, I looked different. I had a traveller's purpose, I thought.

The train was vast and green and dark with two red tail lamps at the back, high above me. A porter came alongside. Carry your bag, he said, you're a foreigner, aren't you? I want to ask how he knew, but before I could shape the question he said, it's the look in the eyes; an innocence. Now I wonder, did he say that? Did I mishear, or did he give voice to my own fears? Even now, when everything else is scratched into my conscience, I cannot be sure of this conversation. No thank you, I said stiffly. I was absurdly proud, although my carriage was right down the platform and the backpack was cutting into my shoulders. I can carry it easily. Suit yourself, he shrugs. I lumbered on.

There was a woman by the door of the carriage. She was wearing a trench mac with railway badges on it and a hat, but underneath the coat she was in tracksuit bottoms and flip-flops. She took my ticket and I boarded and found my compartment. As I passed her little room at the end of the corridor I saw a man sprawled on the bed, reading a paper and drinking beer from a bottle. He paid me no attention.

I was in a compartment with some other women. They had already laid out all their things and they were standing in the corridor. They greeted me cautiously and motioned that I should go in and make myself at home. I put my bag under the bed and sat down, too shy to go out and join my travel companions.

Eventually the train jolted forward and then rolled slowly out of the station and through a goods yard. The women came back into the compartment and began talking to me. They introduced themselves and then started interrogating me. Doesn't your mother mind you going off like this? There are so many bad people in the world. So many wolves. How come you're on your own and so young? I told them my age. See. A little girl. Will you have some dinner with us? They were already busy laying out food on the table. Take some of ours, they urge. Feed you up. I protested weakly, I had money to eat in the restaurant car and I told them so. At that they fell about laughing: beer and cockroaches is all you will find there. So I ate with them. After we had eaten they changed into tracksuits and hung up the suits and jackets they were wearing. I wondered what the fuss and bother was for. I remained in my old outdoor clothes and my boots, trodden down at the back. They looked askance at that and tutted quietly, although I pretended to ignore them. Then it was bedtime. We unrolled our beds and they smeared creams on their faces in front of the mirror and put nets over their hair before lying down and tugging the blankets over them. I lay down on the top bunk as I was, in my traveller clothes, and dreamed in the blue light of wolves with stretched eyes.

It was a long journey, longer than any journey I had ever made in my life. A whole week in the train. I had yet to find out how time can hang heavy, how the back and limbs can ache when they are not exercised. But the first few days passed comfortably enough. The women looked after me. They scolded me for neglecting myself. A woman's duty is to care for herself. Make the best of herself. I became their occupation. I made no fight. After all, I told myself, I am here to see, to learn. When I was once in the corridor one of the women took my oldest t-shirt out of my bag and darned the holes in the sleeves. She folded it and placed it back in my bag. When the train made a long stop they rebuttoned the coat which I had hastily fastened and tucked my hands up under their arms to keep them warm. I dangled between them. What do you want to buy? Bread? Come with us. Pie? This girl here, they told an old woman with a steaming bucket of pies, is foreign. Give her your best pie. The woman unblinkingly held up a pie on a fork. This one is good enough for the Queen of Sheba. Your foreigner can try this. When once the train started moving without us they hoisted me up into the carriage like a rag doll. And they fed me and fed me. Go on, take another. Try this one. With this. Put them together. They themselves picked at the food like sparrows. I couldn't see why they had brought so much, bothered so much – everything homemade and wrapped in towels and newspaper.

When they talked with me they asked me questions, but when they wanted to discuss their own matters they spread the table with food for me and then spoke in slightly lowered voices. Sometimes they went out into the corridor and talked to the men in the carriage. They talked slyly and knowingly to the men; they leant up against the rail and flexed one flip-flop and smiled. At these times they didn't look at me. But I stared at them. I stared at their thin backs and the narrow tops of their arms and their golden shepherd's crook earrings. To see, to learn.

Have you got a boyfriend, they asked me. No. Well then. You must be waiting for Prince Charming. And what do you think of our men? I wondered then if I should be honest. No, that wouldn't do. Load of mummy's boys, down to the very last one, said one woman bitterly. Useless. Utter wastes of space. I'd steer well clear. Lucky for you, you can. We're stuck with them. And they looked at me in a way which made me feel wretched in my state of prolonged childishness. My own unattractiveness to the opposite sex was reflected clear in their faces, in a sort of wry twist to the mouth, a suppressed female superiority.

When they asked me where I was going I told them. But why? They were bewildered. I said that I was going there for the journey and I would look around and then come back. Look around? Around what? I can tell that at those moments I seemed so exotic and peculiar to them I might as well have three heads. Exotic and also slightly insulting in my lack of cares. They had saved their money to come on this train, their few savings. Their worn purses were full of coins which they spent liberally on each other and me, but the notes they kept folded away. It was very cheap for me here. I had a money belt under my shirt with enough money for six such journeys and I made journeys like this for fun. I must have seemed like Alice in Wonderland.

I didn't see the carriage attendant very much. She collected money for the sheets and locked the toilets when we reached a big town, but otherwise stayed in her own compartment with the man. He came out to wash occasionally and stalked the corridor in a vest and tracksuit trousers with a towel around his neck. He, like everyone else, adopted a state of torpor for long periods, staring out of the window or at a newspaper with unseeing eyes. Even the women did this. They reminded me of hummingbirds, open-eyed and frozen, existing at the lowest emotional burn possible until they caught my own eye regarding them. Then they nodded at me in a way both questioning and affirming and looked back at the patience cards or the book they neglected some hours ago. I stretched, shifted, tried to get comfortable, peeked under the curtains at the window. The first days I stared out, but I stopped bothering after that. Snow fell, more and more, and covered the railway embankments and filled the sky. There was always a line of trees running alongside the train, and occasionally the line broke to reveal a mainly flat white plain. A telegraph wire looped up and down endlessly and monotonously.

We seemed to pass all the landmarks at night – a mountain range, a lake. By day it was always the same line of trees. The women hardly looked out at the landscape. Only once: one of them was plaiting my hair. She had a wooden comb and little ribbons. Let me, she said. I'll make it look beautiful for you. I sat facing the window and felt her light fingers moving across my scalp. What a miserable beauty, she said suddenly and I started. The land. Our land. Beautiful, but miserable. I haven't seen it for so long. You notice these things when you haven't been back for this long. I asked her where she has been. She said that she was living in the South with her husband and her little boy but she was returning to her parents now. For good? Yes, for good. There is a war there now. Yes, although she wasn't fighting anyone it happened that her husband and son were on the other side and so they gave her money and told her to go. Your own husband? Your own son? Yes, she said. Doesn't the green ribbon suit you. You should wear that colour. You keep it. Why don't you try my lipstick, too?

I wear the green ribbon. They gave me other little gifts: the wooden comb, a painted figure. I rooted around in my backpack and found nothing of any worth or prettiness to give them in return. I lay on my bunk at night wide awake and rolled the little figure in my hand and wondered about things. Somehow the other passengers managed to sleep at night, even though we did nothing all day. I lay awake. From time to time we passed through a town and floodlights swept across the pale faces. The lips, pouted in sleep, the gold flashing in mouths and ears, the shadows under their eyes. Sometimes the train stopped at night and a man came along the train with a hammer, tapping the wheels rhythmically. There was always a loudspeaker, voices shouting. I did not know what they were saying. Then the train jolted and slid away and we were back in the white desert with the rising falling telegraph wire. And I lay there thinking for hours, wondering about all sorts of things which had never occurred to me before. These thoughts moved in and out of my mind in an unsettling way. They unpicked the loosening seams of my purpose and disappeared again.

At last the women were getting off the train. There was only one more day left of the journey and many of the passengers were already gone. We drank to our friendship with some brandy I bought on a station platform. The four of us drank and lowered glasses, smacking our lips. Then one woman coughed, wiping her mouth with her hand, and motioned for me to pour her some more. I poured another round. They drank to me with a long elaborate speech about how I had become a daughter to them. I wrote my address on three scraps of paper and illustrated them with little stick drawings of all of us. We have grown very fond of you, they said. How we wish we could come with you further, but this is our home. They began describing their town. It was a big town with large slagheaps on one side. The sun rises over the slagheaps and they wished I could see that, as it was particularly beautiful. People who get married in their town go to the top of the slagheaps after the wedding and drink champagne – the view from there is extraordinary as the land itself is flat beyond belief. By the evening of the next day they would be back in their tiny lighted flats around kitchen tables and I would still be on the train. I envied them that. The motionless little table, the food and bottles, a welcome meal.

Still my envy was mixed with incredulity – How can these women be at ease so many miles away from anything? I suppose now I meant, how could they live so far away from civilisation, capital cities. The West, perhaps. My house. These thoughts were vague in my mind. They pressed generally on my understanding; they affected the way my eyes work: when once the train passed over a large river I pointed and watched it rushing away. Where does it go to? Oh that – that is a big river. There are lots of towns and cities along that river, said one woman. A shiver ran down my spine. How can anyone settle so far from the middle of the earth? I am medieval, I scolded myself. I act as if I believed that the world was flat and round like a disc, with me at its centre. I tried to explain a little of this to the women, to mock myself – but it came out very serious and to my surprise the women agreed. For them, too, this was the very rim of the earth. Their families had been sent there. They lived in the same blocks as the local people, but they were not of them. The local people had an accent, they ate differently and they often squatted to piss in the yard in full view of passers-by. They agreed that my home had to be closer to the centre of the earth. This notion was at once flattering and suspicious to me. I smiled, but felt tricked, like a child.

The women told me that they had asked the carriage attendant to look after me and make sure I came to no harm on the last day of my journey. Then I went to bed as they bade me and they waited up because their stop was late at night. We will not wake you, they said. Let's say our goodbyes now. But I insisted. Please wake me. They smiled and kissed me goodnight.

I woke up late at night. There was no one there and all the bags had gone. On the table I saw a little folded piece of paper. There was shouting and laughing from the compartment next door, which had been empty. New passengers. I could hear glasses and bottles being clinked and a loud drunken conversation. I reached down and groped for the note. It read: goodbye and good luck, perhaps we shall meet again, and their names. Underneath the note was a bar of children's chocolate with a fairytale picture on the paper. I snapped off a piece of chocolate and ate it in my loneliness and independence. Then I fell asleep again.

Later I woke up. Now it was quiet in the train, apart from the gentle incessant sound of the wheels on the rails and my hanging coat tapping against the wall. I needed to go to the toilet. Could I wait? I couldn't wait. I climbed down and put on my boots. I was only wearing my long old t-shirt, but there was no-one around to see me. As I passed the next compartment I saw in the dim light a man sleeping fully dressed, his mouth open and his head lolling back. The other bunk was made up, but crumpled and empty. When I reached the toilet at the end of the carriage I heard someone smoking and shuffling about in the unheated outer part of the carriage beyond the toilet. I hesitated, and then I went into the toilet. As I did so I heard the smoker opening the door to come back into the carriage. I turned to shut the toilet door, but the smoker moved suddenly. He kicked at the toilet door and it swung open. I could smell cigarette smoke and drink, but I could not see him. He loomed over me. Now I noticed that he was wearing fatigues and a t-shirt. He grabbed my arm with his hand and I saw he had a tattoo on the webbed piece of skin between thumb and index finger. I didn't dare look into his face. He wrestled with me, pushed me against the metal basin hard, put his hand down to lift the long foolish t-shirt.

I do not understand what happened next. Someone was outside, kicking the door down. It was the carriage attendant's man in his tracksuit, pale with sleep. He took the man by his hair and dragged him backwards, out of the toilet. He was hitting him. I had never heard that sound before. He dragged him out to the outer part of the carriage and then I heard the heavy door opening. There was a sudden shrieking. It blew past the window of the toilet and faded quickly. The door slammed shut. The carriage attendant's man passed me and went wearily back to his attendant, without stopping to ask how I was. The corridor was deserted again – all I could hear were the train's wheels clacking over joins in the track. I was squatting in the toilet with my hands over my ears. When I finally stood I saw the little green ribbon on the floor. I bent to pick it up, but it was lying in the piss and dirt which had washed out of the toilet bowl and I thought better of it. On my way back to my compartment I noticed bloodstains on the wall, smeared and red on the white Formica.

I slept then and wondered when I woke in the morning if I was perhaps dreaming. But the blood was still there on the wall when I went to wash. We were arriving that day. The attendant was collecting bed linen and crockery from the compartments. I heard her next door arguing with the man. He was insisting that he was with another man when he got on the train, and she was insisting, equally firmly, that she had not seen anyone else that morning. She passed my compartment. I called, I have something here for you. She looked in and her face softened, you shouldn't have… Then she realised that I was simply holding out a glass to her and she seized it and marched on. Her man was still in her compartment, lying stretched out and reading a paper. I packed my few things and waited for the city to grow out of the desert. It did so slowly: roads and suburbs, factories and schools, and then finally the goods yards and sheds around the opening to the station.

That night I stayed in a hotel. It was a hotel for foreigners and down in the bar a man was singing into a microphone. He was singing 'Michelle' by the Beatles, but he didn't know the words, so he slurred and ran the foreign sounds together: *mishal mahgull… Ahluvyu, ahluvyu, ahluvyu…* I listened to him. There were plenty of foreign businessmen in the bar. They were sitting around little tables in ones and twos and talking to ladies in high heels and low-cut blouses. I watched them carefully. I remember that it struck me as strange that these respectable businessmen in sober grey suits should have such glamorous colleagues and that they should pay them so much attention.

That next day was bright. I wandered aimlessly, admired the ice sculpture in the square, visited the small local museum. It was full of little tents made from animal skins, and nets and harpoons. Independent and all alone I wandered the avenues. The city was bordered by a wide and powerful river, covered in ice and snow. Down by the river a cold air came off the ice and I could see my own breath more distinctly than ever before. I looked out across the flat space where the water should run – there was another country on the other side, a different people. It looked uninhabited over there, but as dusk fell that day and I watched steadily I could see lights coming on: streetlamps; windows; car headlights; millions and millions of lights.

A Poem by Myra Schneider

Letter from Birsay

Because you've never stood on this beach,
never breathed in this sea, I'll describe the sheet
after sheet of rock compressed into tilted layers,
the stones, bleached orange and ice blue,
lying in heaps and straggles, the ribboning sand,
the causeway leading to the island's green mound.

Because you will not visit this shore, because
you wouldn't see what I do if you did, I want you
to know how the smell of lime weed and salt
jumps me to a beach where water seeped into
our soft castles as we scrambled over rocks, knelt
to capture sleeping crabs and squirming eels.

Although this place trekked by pilgrims who want
to climb to the island's church and look at outlines
of Viking houses, is miles to the north of the one
we shared, although we've lived decades in terrains
so apart no path could link them, on this beach
I half believe the one from long ago is in reach.

Although you misread, misunderstand me – neither
of us is in tune with the other's language – I am writing
to tell you how the sea scoops shells as it sweeps
over sand, wipes out the causeway, drowns rocks
and how, in spite of the dividing water, the island
is stitched to this shore fast as finger to hand.

Dogs in Tolstoy

Brian Nellist

Saul Bellow's Herzog, in one of the imaginary letters he writes to famous people, wants to tell General Eisenhower at the height of the Cold War that the essential quality we should defend is freedom; for Tolstoy, he says, 'That man is free whose condition is simple, truthful – real. To be free is to be released from historical limitation.' Herzog himself is condemned by the misfortunes of his life to be complex, imaginative, even paranoid, but also to learn that he is representative of his time, subject to 'historical limitation'. But he always aspires beyond that condition and, in that, he is rather like Tolstoy himself. For Tolstoy, the figures who come closest to that life of truthful simplicity are, ironically, the people least 'free' in their historically imposed conditions, the peasants or serfs tied to the land and their owners. In an argument with his friend Pierre in *War and Peace*, Andrew Bolkonsky doubts whether Pierre's desire to change the life of his serfs will increase human happiness: 'It seems to me that animal happiness is the only happiness possible.' Freedom is not a state of facing no limitations – that is death – but of *meeting* the demands life makes. It is not bad faith or even social complacency that makes the intellectual Prince Andrew half envy the 'animal happiness', at least the physical contentment, of the peasant whose labour he knows would destroy him:

> 'I go to bed after two in the morning, thoughts come and I can't sleep but toss about till dawn, because I think and can't help thinking, just as he can't help ploughing and mowing.'

The life of conscious thought, by definition, cannot meet its own demands but constantly creates its own dissatisfactions. At least ploughing and mowing can actually be brought to a conclusion with measurable satisfaction. No wonder Levin in *Anna Karenina* envies the completedness of such activity and goes to work in the mowing field.

Even more than the peasant, dogs in Tolstoy's novels exhibit the life that is 'simple, truthful – real'. In the terrible retreat from

Moscow, Pierre, now a prisoner of the French, finds consolation in the endurance, generosity of spirit and inner serenity of a peasant, Platon Karataev, but also of a stray dog with half a dozen names, including Grey. It exhibits an exuberance of spirit, a capacity for play, which affects both the prisoners and their no less captive captors:

> Its furry tail stood up fair and round as a plume, its bandy legs served it so well that it would often gracefully lift a hind leg and run very easily and quickly on three legs, as if disdaining to use all four. Everything pleased it. Now it would roll on its back, yelping with delight, now bask in the sun with a thoughtful air of importance, and now frolic about playing with a chip of wood or a straw.

'Nature is content with only a little' says the old proverb. This is a stray that probably never had an owner, is of no recognisable breed, but is happy to have found this great straggling line of men for the sake of company, the odd tit-bit and the satisfaction of its insatiable sense of curiosity about life. Pierre learns more from Karataev and this dog about the right way to live than from all his previous earnest enquiries. Freedom lies in the right response to the moment and what comes from within a man, and he learns that in his captivity.

It is when he is overtaken by events and sees in others, including a dumb brute, how to cope with them that Pierre starts thinking well. As Newman writes in a very different context, 'Life is for action. If we insist on proofs for everything we shall never come to action; to act you must assume and that assumption is faith.' Tolstoy's dogs certainly think but they think in and to the moments that arise; their motto would be 'Here and Now', whereas their owners are distracted by the pride and expectation they invest in their animals. In the great wolf-hunt in *War and Peace*, Nicholas Rostov, the most practical of the three young men whose careers span the novel, has gone to hunt on land adjoining that of an elderly poor relation called, with affectionate disrespect, 'Uncle'. They join forces with the borzois of another neighbour, Ilagin. Nicholas' pride in the family pack is already clear when his old hound, Karay, downs a wolf in 'the happiest moment of Nicholas' life'. But, defensive of Milka, the pride of his kennels, he at once identifies a rival in Erza, one of Ilagin's hounds:

> a small, pure-bred, red-spotted bitch of Ilagin's, slender but with muscles like steel, a delicate muzzle and prominent black eyes.

A judge at Crufts could do no better. Yet when they pit the dogs against each other against a hare, Erza is fastest, but in over-eagerness, falls head over tail in her haste. Milka overshoots the quarry when the hare suddenly squats and it is 'Uncle's' red hound, Rugay, who is never described for his good looks, who seizes the prey. For the dog, as for man, what matters in the end is not abstract capacity but practical skill. Rugay shows judgement, wisdom, what Newman, following Aristotle, calls 'phronesis'. The baffled richer sportsmen look quizzically at 'Uncle's' dog:

> For a long time they continued to look at red Rugay who, his arched back spattered with mud and clanking the ring of his leash, walked along just behind 'Uncle's' horse with the serene air of a conqueror.
>
> 'Well, I am like any other dog as long as it's not a question of coursing. But when it is, then look out!' his appearance seemed to Nicholas to be saying.

It's this instinct and the action that discloses the dog, not the perfection of shape in repose. That serenity of living happily, truly, within its skin is to be recalled later in the novel by Pierre's grey mongrel.

Tolstoy was a sportsman, but his interest in hunting, shooting and coursing is no more an end in itself in the novels than any of the other details of existence which teem in his pages. The real interest lies in how man and dog collaborate in the oldest of human activities, hunter-gathering. The great French naturalist, Buffon, had argued in the eighteenth century that, 'The first art of mankind was the education of dogs and the fruit of this art was the conquest and peaceful possession of the earth'. The strategies of human intelligence combine with the tactical nous of the beast. The dog, however, always knows what it wants, but human beings are distracted by reflection and emotion. In *Anna Karenina*, Levin returns to his estate having been rejected by Kitty Shcherbatsky but is joined months later by Oblonsky (Stiva), married to Kitty's sister, Dolly. They go off to shoot woodcock and snipe, together with Laska, the retriever. Levin learns that Kitty is not married to Vronsky, as he had assumed, but is gravely ill. At that moment a woodcock rises but Laska thinks only of the job in hand:

> 'What a time they have chosen to talk,' thought she. 'And there it comes flying … Just so, here it is. They'll miss it …'

'There', 'here'; Laska lives in time, undisturbed by anxieties about which one can do nothing. But both men, in tune with the dog, react spontaneously and down the bird. Only when he is collecting it does Levin then remember 'Ah! But there was something unpleasant … Yes, of course, Kitty is ill … Found? Good dog.' This is not a satire on the failure of priorities or on the heartlessness of sportsmen, but an instance of how animal instinct works independently of profound emotion. Healthily, our world does not stop when we grieve and the 'Good dog' coexists with 'something unpleasant'.

For Tolstoy, Francis Bacon's image – that Man stands in relation to the dog as God to himself and that the animal is better for its subservience – simply does not apply. Though the sportsman has still more power over the dog than he has over his serfs, in both cases the relationship does not work unless it is collaborative. In a later shoot with Oblonsky, Levin is thrown out of his rhythm by a bumptious tyro, a relation of his wife, Kitty. Then, when he does manage to shoot a bird,

> Laska was incredulous of his having killed anything and when he sent her to look for it, she only made a pretence and did not really search.

The dogs pick up their masters' emotions, so although Oblonsky, who has had a good day, considerately suppresses his glee, his own dog has no such reserve:

> Krak, quite black with fetid marsh slime, sprang out from beneath the upturned root of an alder with the air of a conqueror and sniffed Laska.

Yet stealing a march by rising early before the others next day, Levin recovers his spontaneous confidence. Laska uses her nose to identify snipe but, with his human height, Levin, once Laska has pointed, can actually see the bird beyond the hummock that hides it from the dog. He forces her forward against her nature, using her like a springer to start the game:

> 'But I can't go,' thought she. 'Whom should I go to? From here I scent them, but if I go forward I shall not know what I'm doing nor where they are.'
>
> But now he pushed her with his knee, saying in an excited whisper, 'Seize it Laska! Seize it!'
>
> 'Well, if he wishes it I will, but I can no longer answer for anything,' thought Laska and rushed forward at full tilt between the hummocks. She now scented nothing more, but only saw and heard without understanding anything.

Master and dog are a unity, he with his sight, she with her scent. The dog does not simply lose her identity by obeying beyond her instincts. Her protest is entered: 'I can no longer answer for anything.' But, as Newman would have it, she acts on the assumption that is an act of faith in the newly-confident Levin. She goes 'at full tilt' beyond what she can understand. In *The Republic* Plato's Socrates, admittedly with a smile, maintains that dogs are true philosophers because they love learning to know new people, to admit them to friendship, but also for Tolstoy, even when as experienced as Laska, to learn new tricks. It is important in novels so much concerned with thinking about the problems of life that, included in the varieties of thought, there should be that of dogs. They are not simply reflexive engines as Descartes imagined, but creatures with independent minds, rooted in their faith in their masters, but beyond the complexities of human intelligence, for better and worse, 'simple, truthful – real'.

Two Poems by
Elena Shvarts
translated by Sasha Dugdale

By the Pantheon

On the square where the Pantheon's
Curved flank gleams purple
Like a giant's mighty skull
Like a migraine-pulsed temple
Where juice, damp roses
Are handed out by mulattos –
There I watched the archness
Of dolphins, then left
Into the Pantheon's strange dusk
The dome of its forehead.

The quiet simmering of the sky
In a vague January sun –
Blueing above me
The hole of the Pantheon
Like the Cyclops' naked eye
Day's sea-blue, at evening
It mists over, at night
A star grinds the grey sand.
I went out and at the entrance
A beggar wrapped in a blanket
And Bernini's little elephant
Saddled by cruel midday
As if to ride out his trophy
For Roman winter play
Then I saw it was an honour –
In a moment it struck home:
It is Rome's indifference
To all that is not Rome.

Gogol on the Spanish Steps

And Rome is still the back of beyond…
The forum is still grazed by goats
And a tiny monkey by the name of Chi-chi
Frowning, turns a barrel organ's crank.
Here, at the foot of the Spanish steps
Died Keats not long ago.
A spring day, and from via Felice
A man with a stoop and a long nose
Skips down the steps with such joy
Like a goldcrest or a golden-eye.
Now and then he steals a sidelong glance
At the shadow's tricorn
With its bag over its shoulder.
And dead souls lying in the bag
Pleading to be let out.
But this tricorn, this man
Of a respectable and shadowy age
A limitless, boundless age
Runs sideways, fan-like, down the steps.
And oh, he will not relent until death.
An artist ascends towards him
And waves, buon giorno, Nicolà!
But he in answer only abruptly smiles
And brushes off someone behind.
The tiny monkey by the name of Chi-chi
Gazes moistly, a new coin in its hand.

Reading Scott

Bernard Beatty

A copy of Scott's *The Talisman* was lying round the house when I was a child, and since I tended to read everything that was around, I read it. I remember some scenes still – Scott can always do this – but I did not much take to it. I thought that I did not like Scott. I next tried about twelve years later when I was a postgraduate writing a thesis on Byron. I thought that I ought to read Scott, partly because Byron had done so. I read the long poems with respect and pleasure and then tried *Waverley*. I found the opening of the novel difficult – most new readers of Scott find the opening pages of his novels the hardest task – but came both to enjoy and admire it. I think I read *The Bride of Lammermoor* at about the same time. I began to think that Scott was considerably underrated and probably read Georg Lukács's brilliant Marxist account of Scott in his *The Historical Novel* then too, but that was as far it went. Later still I found myself teaching Scott's *Old Mortality*, was influenced by discussions with my then colleagues (Vince Newey, Brian Nellist, Steve Newman), and more or less had a conversion to him. At that time I read about twenty of his novels in the space of perhaps two or three years and have re-read the ones set in Scotland – commonly and correctly regarded as by far the best ones – many times since then.

Why did it take such a long time for me to learn how to enjoy Scott and get on the right wavelength to read him? Partly it is a simple matter – it is not a good idea to begin with an author's second best works. Mainly, it is a matter of having too clear expectations of what a book should be like before reading it. Scott does not do lots of things that we have come to expect and to require in a novel. He is not, for instance, very interested in sex, which has increasingly become the main subject matter of modern novels. He does not hide the transitions from one scene to another that writers like Flaubert or even Dickens are at great pains to handle with great tact. In a similar way, he affronts our own sense of sophistication by giving us the sort of adventures that seem to belong in the world of children's stories or Steven Spielberg. Worse still, he neither gives us a realistic world nor one which we can regard as a self-enclosed dream fiction. There is too much history for it to be fiction and too much fiction for it to be history. In his Scots novels (*Waverley*, *Old Mortality*, *The Bride of Lammermoor*, *Rob Roy*, *Guy Mannering*, *The Antiquary*, *The Heart of Midlothian*, *Redgauntlet*), much of the dialogue is in Broad Scots and most of his readers find it difficult to follow. The style of the narrative itself is in rather laborious sub-Johnsonian English. He is not much interested in the changing role of women. We cannot, with him, easily play the critical game of 'who is narrating?' without which so many 'intelligent' critiques of the novel would never get going. He wrote rapidly for money. He left the business of punctuation and even larger acts of editing to his publishers as no self-respecting 'great artist' should. He is never primarily interested in the interior experience of his central characters. Most heinous of all, he was on the Right in politics. In other words, he robs us of nearly all our accustomed ways of reading, thinking, and talking about novels and artists. Yet there is no question that Scott is a great writer, that he shows us important things that no other writer does so well, and that he is compulsively enjoyable to read. He enlarges and changes our attitudes to life, art, space, and time. He 'sees' (Ruskin's great word of praise for a writer) more than most writers and more than most men.

Why did I change my mind about Scott? The first time that I got an inkling of Scott's greatness, and also of what fun it is to read him, was in the opening sections of one of his long poems – *The Lady of the Lake*. We tend to forget how widely these poems were read and their enormous effects on, for instance, the Brontës. In the opening scene, there is an intensely realised description of a stag hunt. Scott describes hunting brilliantly. It is as good as the scenes in *Gawain and the Green Knight* or *Tom Jones*. The ethics of hunting are neither here nor there. What first interests Scott is sharing habitual consciousness with other kinds of consciousness – here that of an animal. There are cross-overs between the two. The hunter finds himself alone, his horse run into the ground, brought by the stag into unknown and strange country which the stag is at home in and he is not. What is impressive is the suddenness of the rider's loss of authority and the absolute authority of the new world in which he finds himself, which seems to need no underpinning. We believe we are where we are and we gaze with a pure simplicity of vision on a world of absolute strangeness which is nevertheless our world. The stag is written out. His purpose was simply to bring us here:

> The western waves of ebbing day
> Roll'd o'er the glen their level way;
> Each purple peak, each flinty spire,
> Was bathed in floods of living fire.
> …

> No pathway meets the wanderer's ken
> ...
> From the steep promontory gazed
> The stranger, raptured and amazed.
> ...
> From underneath an aged oak,
> That slanted from the islet rock
> A damsel guider of its way,
> A little skiff shot to the bay
> ...
> The boat had touch'd this silver strand,
> Just as the hunter left his stand,
> And stood conceal'd amid the brake,
> To view this Lady of the Lake.

Over and over again in Scott's novels, something like this occurs. A familiar world is displaced by an unfamiliar one which in turn becomes familiar to us and yet retains its strangeness. Like the surprised hunter, we are 'raptured and amazed' by the rapidity with which we have been thrust into the marvellous but we view what is in front of us steadily for it is solid and substantial and the place of unexpected real incident ('shot to the bay'). This is the stuff of an adventure story, of travel (most of Scott's main characters spend much time travelling), but also of growing up, ageing, and – more largely still – of life itself and all historical change. In the great Scots novels, the movement from familiar Southern England to unfamiliar far north, or from Lowlands to Highlands, is also a movement in time, for we are entering a world which preserves forms of actions and consciousness which the later world has forgotten. In this way, what the hero does (it is always a hero, with the exception of Jeanie Deans in *The Heart of Midlothian*) mimics what the reader is doing. *Waverley*, the first of them, is also the classic case. Its sub-title is ''Tis Sixty Years Since', for it is set during the Jacobite uprising of 1745 but written for a Regency audience. They (and we) look back to an earlier time when Edward Waverley is reading about an earlier time through his passion for Romance literature and then finds himself caught up in the still semi-feudal world of the Highlands and the apparent attempt to restore that world through the figure of Bonnie Prince Charlie. The attempt fails and Waverley returns to his own modern world just as the reader does when the exciting book is finally put down. But it is more complicated and interesting than that. The modern world of Waverley and the reader has partly been created by the events which we are reading about. New futures are often created by attempts to restore versions of the past. Imagining effects historical change though imagined worlds are never directly realised. Scott reads the post-Reformation history of Modern Scotland like this and sees in it the model of all history.

In the same way, when one of Scott's heroes enters a strange world, he enters both a space governed by time and vice versa. Bakhtin, who wrote on Scott, coined the rather ugly word 'chronotope' for this fusion of space and time which we have, since Einstein, become increasingly accustomed to. Scott's novels are the human equivalent of Einstein's physics here.

I have emphasised strangeness, but this is only one half of the story. It is the half which aligns Scott with Romanticism roughly speaking. Ruskin's 'Seer' had two senses. On the one hand it is the prophetic vision to see beyond the everyday, but it is also to see what is under our noses directly rather than what we have been accustomed to thinking that we see. If Scott shocks his heroes with the unfamiliar, he shocks his readers by his fidelity to the given in all, or nearly all, its forms. He knows many different landscapes, weathers, times of day and night. He is familiar with the ways of all classes (very rare in modern literature). He likes pedants, gossips, lawyers, gypsies, and old women as much as soldiers, queens, and poets. He can describe a sermon, those who listen to it, the building it takes place in, the effect it has, as well as a fight in a cave or an assignation by a waterfall. He is usually sympathetic to all his characters because he always shows the history and place that has made them what they are but he is capable of bitter and bleak rejections. He is superb in listening to conversations – familiar ones between those who know one another well and wary ones, with something of the animal about them, between those who are guessing at the consciousness of others. 'Wary' because the right or wrong words in conversation can cause action. There is a splendid example of this in Chapter XV of *The Heart of Midlothian*. Again it is difficult to quote in part. One of Scott's great dramatic creations – Madge Wildfire, a once beautiful, now deranged, gypsy – is being interrogated by an astute procurator (Sharpitlaw) and a criminal turned informer (Ratcliffe). Scott's names, like those of Dickens, usually indicate character. The interrogation hangs on judgements which both reader and interrogators are making as to Madge's sanity but also on the awkward relationship between the interrogators which is disclosed by the gap between directness and indirectness, represented partly by the distance between inherited styles of active language and less assured kinds of calculated role-play. Both Scott and the reader delight in the way crazy Madge is sharper than Sharpitlaw, who in turn is not as cunning as Ratcliffe, who tricks Madge indirectly into larger self-disclosure:

> 'I dinna believe a word o't,' said Ratcliffe, with another wink to the procurator. 'Thae duds were a' o' the colour o'moonshine in the water, I'm thinking Madge – The gown wad be a sky-blue-scarlet, I'se warrant ye?'
>
> 'It was nae sic thing,' said Madge, whose unretentive memory let out, in the eagerness of contradiction, all that she would have most wished to keep concealed, had her judgement been equal to her inclination. 'It was neither scarlet nor sky-blue, but my ain auld brown threshie-coat of a short gown, and my mother's auld mutch, and my red rokelay – and he gied me a croun and a kiss for the use o' them, blessing on his bonny face – though it's been a dear ane to me.'
>
> 'And where did he change his clothes again, hinnie?' said Sharpitlaw, in his most conciliatory manner.
>
> 'The procurator's spoiled a',' observed Ratcliffe drily. And it was even so; for the question, put in so direct a shape, immediately awakened Madge to the propriety of being reserved upon those topics on which Ratcliffe had indirectly seduced her to become communicative.
>
> 'What was't ye were speering at us, sir?' she resumed, with an appearance of stolidity so speedily assumed, as showed there was a great deal of knavery mixed with her folly.

Speech here is brimful of life, risk, and the play of directness and indirectness that discloses personality and shapes event. That is why Scott is less interested in introspection than many nineteenth-century writers and why Ruskin is right to align him with Homer. We are not simply faithful to experience by describing our interior lives or describing the exterior worlds in which we find ourselves. Both interior and exterior worlds are constantly changing and these changes are brought about through words and actions. Words are a form of action as well as a mode of self-expression. This is the whole point of Ratcliffe's manoeuvre which traps Madge into revealing hidden facts through her spontaneous desire for self-expression. We find ourselves pitched at birth into a landscape, a language, an already formed but still changing history. We come to the knowledge of words and events together. These are not other than us, they make us what we are, but what we are is always changing. We change the world and the world changes us. Scott understands this and shows this more than any other writer of fiction. Sociology and psychology are the bane of art, and the death of criticism. Sociology transfers structures from history into one-dimensional intellectual space. Psychology thins out the make-up of a consciousness into familiar diagnostic forms. Scott gives us neither for we live in real space and time which can be shown but never 'caught' and which neither exist separately from us, for we shape them, nor are simply 'constructed' by us. Scott's novels show us real space and time but don't claim to 'catch' them. Instead he makes his readers be caught up in the worlds that he shows them but keeps us always aware that they are 'made up'. The distinction between reality and imagination is real to him but not absolute, determinative or crucifying as it is for Keats or Shelley.

The structure of Scott's novels is complicated and often lumpy. Plot and story are not usually the same thing. *Redgauntlet* – to my mind the greatest of all his achievements – bewilders and bamboozles the reader, not least by interpolating an enormous short story halfway through. But they all work towards marriage or the denial of marriage and we read the structures as a whole in order to understand them. The novels are not about marriage in the sense that Jane Austen's are (Scott much admired her and admitted that she could do things that he could not). Austen is interested in the ground of possibility for good marriage which depends upon the right sensibility and the right judgements made by individuals. Individuals are formed by society but the major emphasis in Austen falls the other way – society depends upon the right choices made by individuals. Marriage is the place where both meet and marriage is best when it is between those who share and understand the same values. The great enemy is selfishness and the instability which it brings about. Scott is not interested in this. He is interested in the great instabilities which form the dynamism of history and the alliances between opposites which give temporary but real shape to periods of history and social and religious forms. Marriage is through the attraction of opposites which is both heterosexuality and the dialectical structure of all events. This can be read positively (for human lives and social forms exist, can be comely and we love them) or negatively (for every new form destroys an old one and can thus never be relied on nor wholly believed in). In *The Bride of Lammermoor* and *Redgauntlet* Scott gives us grimly negative readings of human affairs and there are always lurking signs of this bleakness in the positive novels but he is on both sides of the fence always. In this, he offers a sort of wisdom to us which could not be summed up in a sentence or two.

Yes I like Scott. Indeed I love him. If you don't like the opening pages of one of his novels, just keep reading anyway. *Old Mortality* and *The Bride of Lammermoor* (which worked for me) are still perhaps the best way in. Don't attempt *Redgauntlet* until you have read three or four of the others. If you read enough Scott novels, they tell you how to read him.

Three Poems by Kate Keogan

Madonna Col Bambino

Looking back, it was unmistakable –
The unquenched taste in the mouth, just like blood;
Or, as Virgil taught, the coin under tongue,
Charon's wages. The Ferryman.
Newly arrived in Venice – a city
Like nothing I can recollect of life –
I'm bewildered, by myself not least of all.
For I have slipped the rope of the self
That I had believed to be my all
And now am brinking deeper waters,
With an altered name, a two-days' husband
And new life ahead, within, beckoning me.
So the gondola might be a chrysalis,
Cocooning me, as my mouth fills with blood
Of a self I outgrew and stretched to split.
And throughout the day the delicate
Stirring I felt, like moth-wings beaten,
The welcome ache of minute subdivision.

We embarked as night began softly to fall
And the lights on the Bridge of Sighs
Bled and were haloed in the thickened air.
The next day we are back in Verona,
At the Castelvecchio (where Dante
Spent his exile) and it is cold still
But I'm close to fainting, as I grope for the window,
For the light blazing through it undeterred.
I'm certain now, and burn to proclaim it
But am too shy yet to tell even my husband,
For we are looking at paintings
Of the Virgin Mary; the ambivalent
Child. She has turned away from me, from him;
She has had her fill of miracles.

In the Garden

Not my only delight, assuredly,
that took by stealth my sleeve
as I set my heart on the fragrance,
the passion, the draught of heaven-breath,
and showed me instead the welling
of my own astonished blood
and said, 'Stay here. Remember.' Said,
'When were you never loved like this?'

Golden Wedding

How sharply everything comes into focus,
now that I have left, the photographs
of them in their twenties at arm's length
from each other on the sideboard:
my Nan, anyone's idea of beauty;
Grandad, recognisably a stranger
smiling beneath his soldier's cap.
One morning stands especially clear
helping Nan in the kitchen:
she gave me the leavings to play with,
shaping pasties out of potato-peelings,
the carrot-tops and greying dough,
silently marking how tenderly
she brought the knife again and again
to meet and rest at her fingertips;
blunted now, of course, after years of use,
still sharp enough to draw blood.

The Practice of Poetry

The Love of Poetry and Looking Closely in W.S. Graham's 'Untidy Dreadful Table'

Adam Piette

When the word 'reader' is spoken without specific reference to what is being read, it is unconsciously assumed that prose fiction is the thing. It is as though readers cannot cope with the attention demands of poetry – or that, fearful of poetry, they'll step gingerly away from any close contact with the genre. Shortcomings in culture and teaching are often blamed, but it has to be acknowledged that poetry as an institution is partly at fault if only for not preserving the contacts with the general public which might have fostered and sustained the forms of education *through reading* which generate genuine love of poetry.

But the argument is circular, in a sense. For poetry as an institution only lost that contact because readers began to assume that poetry was too difficult for them – as a consequence of modernism, surrealism and all that jazz. And that assumption is based on a loss of the specific forms of attention required by most poems. That loss cannot be put entirely at poetry's door, however – for the specific attention can only be acquired if one *reads* poetry. It is a terrible double bind. Poetry gets blamed for being difficult because readers don't read poetry any more because it's too difficult. But poetry can only become accessible if readers read enough of it to grow to love it – that love being exactly the same thing as knowing how to read it, and knowing how to read it comes with simply reading it! Loving poetry *is* reading it. The difficulty lies only in the time it takes to pay loving attention to the words as they come.

A test case might be a poet such as W.S. Graham, who suffered all his life from neglect, yet was sustained by loyal and dedicated friends. Those who took pains to read him learned his style, like a foreign tongue – the loving is in the understanding. His small readership cannot be blamed on Sydney Graham. His work so beautifully imagines tender witty contact and encounter with the reader. But the poetry itself is odd, twisty, quirky, half-crabbed for those only conversant with prose style. It does need the reader's attention – but that is *all* it asks.

Attention is difficult to define, but it is, at its simplest, a slowing down of our reading speed, at least at first, so as to register the things *seen* first of all. Once into the skin of the poem, then it can be inhabited, its little environment learnt, the things it says it sees visualised and understood. Readers need not be afraid – all that is needed is to step into the poem as into somebody's room, and to begin to see with the eyes offered by the poem. It might take a little time to get the room into one's focus, like borrowing someone else's glasses. It might be surprising to realise through whose eyes one *is* looking. But all it takes is time

Untidy Dreadful Table

Lying with no love on the paper
Between the typing hammers I spied
Myself with looking eyes looking
Down to cover me with words.

I won't have it. I know the night
Is late here sitting at my table,
But I am not a boy running
The hide and seeking streets.

I am getting on. My table now
Shuffles its papers out of reach
With last year's letters going yellow
From looking out of the window.

I sit here late and I hammer myself
On to the other side of the paper.
There I jump through all surprises.
The reader and I are making faces.

I am not complaining. Some of the faces
I see are interesting indeed.
Take your own, for example, a fine
Grimace of vessels over the bone.

Of course I see you backwards covered
With words backwards from the other side.
I must tackle my dreadful table
And go on the hide and seeking hill.

Taking the time to see the poem is as simple as working out where it's speaking from and where its 'eyes' are located. Who is doing the seeing in the first stanza? The I is spying on the myself from the paper in the typewriter, one learns. Taking this slowly partly means appreciating the oddity and the joke – letting the joke creep up on you as the lines are read. The poet is writing a poem with the word 'I' in it – his I is therefore hammered onto the page. If we accept the idea, comically here, that a poem can *see*, in the sense that a poem, at its simplest, is a way of seeing as well as a way of talking, or rather a way of seeing as talking, then Graham's joke starts to work on us. If the poet's eye sees then it sees as if from the vantage point of the words typed on the page, and as if looking out on the world – in the first stanza, the world is the actual room the poem is being composed in: Sydney Graham's cottage in Madron, Cornwall in the 1970s.

The slow attention will also catch other comic touches – the playful allusion to the I Spy game (I spy with my little eye) in 'I spied / Myself with looking eyes' (bored poet playing childish games with his persona); the poet's loneliness joked up with reference to all those seduction poems ('Come lie with me and be my love' &c.) in the opening line.

But attention really also means carefully visualising the arrangement of persons and things. If we take time to do this then we release the strange surreal comedy of the thing. One can do this by making the submerged metaphors real in space, by *literalising* them: the 'myself' figure beating away at the I-voice with his hammers, then burying him with words. Or we can do it by trying to get the whole picture in cartoon form in the mind's eye: the wee ghost figure lying on the page being covered with typescript whilst overseen by big brother with his scary gaze.

It's not only the jokes that develop as time is given by the reader to the poem: fear of death is real too here – poems might be mere resting-places for the future dead spirit of W.S. Graham, the 'cover me with words' phrase seems to be hinting. There is slightly deranged *timor mortis* in those 'looking eyes looking'. Graham is imagining himself as an afterlife spirit trapped in typewritten space, perpetually gazed upon by the living eyes he once had in the real world.

The poem is strange, comic, cartoony – but it isn't *difficult*. It's only difficult in the other sense – Graham is being boyish and naughty with his huffy 'I won't have it', his 'I am not a boy' belied by the sulky tone. And there's something charmingly childlike too in the line 'The hide and seeking streets': Graham, brought up on the streets of Greenock where he'd play hide and seek with his pals, living most of his adult life 'abroad' in rural Cornwall, is exiled from his childhood; but that childhood is summoned into being in the very playfulness of the nonce adjective.

Still, once on to the second and third stanzas, we quickly *see* that he has switched back into his real body 'here sitting at my table'. The comic banter has receded and we're left with an old man, fearful of old age (those yellowing letters), lonely without a real feel for his public, his mind wandering and wondering about the real world out there through his window. So old is he that the table and letters seem to have more life than he.

The joke about the separate selves returns in the last three stanzas, this time with a funny twist. Instead of the tired and slightly sinister composing self, the poet's persona (the creature he becomes when constructed by the poem's words) sees the faces of the reader, the many readers dreamt of, and the actual reader – you, yes you, *you* in particular, grimacing at the dark humour of the poem. You the reader are glimpsed through the 'words backwards' as though the persona were peering at you from behind the paper, like a goblin ghost, alive on the other side of the poem's page (the actual page you were holding when you read the poem) punned with the 'other side' of the life-death divide.

The frightening gaze of the composing self is gone and Graham finds a certain black comedy in the idea of looking back at the reader with as unsettling a stare. The stare sees the skull beneath the skin, 'vessels over the bone', the bone of the reader's skull. The X-ray gaze takes us into the old man's *timor mortis* in the ancient ways of all poets – one of the old old tasks of the poet was to remind us of time passing. He is seeing you backwards not only as goblin peering through the back-to-front words of this poem, but also backwards in that ancient sense – Marvell's 'and at my *back* I hear / Time's wingéd chariot hurrying near'; Shakespeare's 'dark *backward* and abyss of time'. Graham's version, 'I see you backwards covered / With words': you too will some day be covered with words as by the dust and the earth, not least by the poem's words hurrying near (too near) to you from the other side, from dear departed Sydney buried on the hide and seeking hill (hiding behind his words, seeking you in his afterlife), seeing you through the words he wrote *to you*, you with your interesting face reading this, here and now, counting backwards towards the other side at dreadful time's table.

Comic, bantering, affectionate, jokey-epistolary, over-familiar but in joshing black humour, the poem sees us only when we take it at its own comic pace, when we choose to see it through, watched as closely by the visible poet if and only if we *lovingly imagine* messy old man Graham looking back at us across the backward and abyss of time, he so hammered when alive, by time, by neglectful readers, by his own doubtful self. A thing of paper and inky words, yet also a voice weirdly alive, waiting for us to look closely, with love. Poetry is as easy as that, as easy as playing hide and seek.

> If you were to destroy in mankind the belief in immortality, not only love but every living force maintaining the life of the world would at once be dried up.
>
> Dostoevsky, from *The Brothers Karamazov*

Reading in Schools

Four pieces on the state of reading in school. Ex-teacher Sharon Connor writes about sixth-formers' relationships with books; Andrew Cunningham examines matters from a current teacher's point of view, while Ed Kirk gives an insight into the student's position. Shelley Bridson gives her lively account of a QCA seminar.

Can Sixth-Formers Read?

Sharon Connor

Sharon Connor, who manages The Reader's programme of events for schools, was invited to speak at a conference on Reading for Pleasure organised by The Guardian *in London on 7 July 2005. Mainly attended by schoolteachers and school librarians, the conference aimed to address issues around the future of reading for pleasure and English teaching in schools. This is an edited transcript of Sharon's speech.*

I first started teaching at Southport College on Merseyside, and when I told the very first group of English AS students I had that we would be reading Charles Dickens' *Hard Times*, some looked horrified and one of the students asked in an amazed voice, 'You want us to read a book, miss?' They had got through their GCSE exams using a combination of short stories or extracts from books. And I – like many others, I imagine, both inside and outside the teaching profession – had misjudged what English means to some students. The assumption I had made was that they had chosen to continue with English in post-compulsory education because they had a real enthusiasm for books, for reading; and in some cases this was absolutely true, but for a frighteningly high percentage of the students in those classes, many just viewed it as a 'good' subject to have on their UCAS forms.

After a couple of years' teaching I had the opportunity to get involved with The Reader's schools project. One of the biggest problems I've encountered here has been teachers' own expectations. The very first full-day event I organised was what we called a 'War Literature' day, looking at not just the standard First World War poetry but anything and everything that connected to conflict. For example, one group looked at Tolstoy's *War and Peace* and another group looked at Shakespeare's *Henry V*. At the end of the day I collected in the feedback forms from the visiting teachers and students, and I was astonished at the variation in responses. One of the teachers filled in her form with these comments: 'Objectives weren't stated, pupils didn't know what to expect. Perhaps you have something to learn from A-level teachers who work to make lessons sharply focused.' These comments troubled me deeply. Could her students only function as readers if they were given an objective to aim for? Why did all lessons have to be *sharply* focused? And then I read the feedback sheet one of her own pupils had completed. She wrote, 'I liked the fact I was able to have my own opinion and that it was taken into account.'

The second example I want to give you comes from a Shakespeare Day. Although the morning sessions were focused on the A-level set texts, the afternoon was to be spent looking at Shakespeare's sonnets, and this was quite a point of contention with some teachers, since the sonnets were not on the reading list of the syllabus they were studying. But I took a hard line and insisted that the sonnets stayed. Again collecting the feedback forms at the end of the day, I was struck by two brief comments from students: 'Can we have more on the sonnets even though I am not studying them?', and 'I enjoyed the session on Shakespeare's sonnets, it was interesting and personal.'

To my mind, these comments from students all add up to the same thing: students might be getting what the English syllabus demands of them, but they're not getting what they need as readers. And this is the point my rather contentious title was trying to make. Are sixth-formers being allowed to read for creative and passionate reasons, or is this being actively discouraged by the aims and objectives of the current A-level coursework and examination system?

To return to my opening question, 'Can sixth-formers read?', it's probably taken for granted that by this stage in their education they most certainly can. But I'm not questioning literacy skills, I'm questioning whether pupils are encouraged to be passionate readers, whether they are allowed to voice their own reaction, not just give a standard textbook response. Last year one of our senior lecturers gave a talk on Marlowe's *Dr Faustus*. A day or two later we received a call from one of the teachers whose group had attended the lecture. He wanted his money back: 'We had already told [the pupils] what they should think but after the lecture they don't know what they should think'. So we have found that it's best not to organise events that are closely tied in with any of the English syllabi. Earlier this week we held a poetry day, and in the weeks beforehand we had a number of teachers asking what sort of texts would be looked at so that they could 'prepare' their students. I wasn't in a position to give them that information, since we leave the choice of materials to individual workshop leaders, but I felt it was quite sad that the teachers felt their students needed to be almost primed for what should be – and was – a creative day.

Having been a teacher myself, I know only too well how difficult working 'outside the box' can be. The relentless pressure that is faced by teachers on a daily basis must fatigue even the most enthusiastic within the profession. I know that targets have to be met, and that many teachers are as much victims of the system as many pupils are. When I did my teacher training I was told that I was a 'facilitator of information'. I think that when we are viewed as little more than robots that churn out information it becomes inevitable that there is the prospect of simply becoming just that – ultimately to the detriment of both staff and students. If this continues, we face the possibility of having a whole generation of English students who can interpret and deconstruct a text, but may never have experienced the sheer joy of reading a book for pleasure.

Is Reading Doomed?

Andrew Cunningham

When you look at the fuss surrounding the launch of the latest Harry Potter book or film, the picture seems rosy. Writers such as Rowling, Pullman and Jacqueline Wilson continue to sell to young children. But should you happen to be present in our classrooms at the end of a summer term, when English teachers tentatively suggest to teenagers that they might like to think about reading a few books over the long holidays, the picture seems one of despair. Howls of teenage derision meet the idea of spending summer time reading.

It's the same bleak picture at parent–teacher meetings for teenagers in schools up and down the land. Parents of all backgrounds continually ask this question: 'Why won't they read? What can we do to encourage them?' The reluctance of teenage boys in particular to read often has nothing to do with class or social background, or with the availability of books in the family home. 'There are loads of books in the house and we've always read as a family but he still won't pick up a book.'

So perhaps a division needs to be drawn between pre-teens, who read avidly, given good books, and many teens who most adamantly won't.

The QCA (the Qualifications and Curriculum Authority) hasn't helped matters. Recently it threw the whole issue of reading classic works in school syllabuses into question. Its review of the shape and future of English in schools by 2015, confusingly called 'English 21', posed this worrying question: will books be part of the formal school curriculum by 2015? 'English 21' even suggested the unthinkable: 'Will the printed book disappear?' The review may have been kicked into touch by a legion of outraged teachers, parents and experts, led by the Poet Laureate himself, who all reaffirmed the sacrosanct place of books in our schools, but worrying times for the printed word could lie ahead.

So much depends upon the books a particular teacher likes and therefore wishes to encourage the young to read. Get the wrong book at the wrong age and you'll put them off for life, whereas well-chosen books may still produce results. Recently I gave a class of fourteen-year-old boys *Right Ho, Jeeves* for holiday reading. They read it, enjoyed it and were full of the book for days after. The language might be dated, the characters redundant: but the comic twists of the plot still held good and still held them. There's a richness in the language that even today's teenagers can latch on to. One or two, unprompted, asked for more Wodehouse.

But there seems to be no real conception, especially amongst teenage boys, that writers such as Austen or George Eliot could be enjoyable. I was shocked when one seventeen-year-old, to whom I'd taught *Persuasion*, confessed that he'd hated this book so much he burnt it after his exams. Such hostile reactions may owe much to bad teaching. But a major handicap books face amongst teenagers like these is the inbuilt resistance to works of length, even when part of the school syllabus. Those great 800-page classics that formed the cornerstone of English Literature for nearly two hundred years are now, in effect, unteachable. Some English A- and AS-level exam boards gamely keep George Eliot's *Middlemarch* on the syllabus. It's a purely tokenist exercise.

Thus, even at good schools with good exam results, when it comes to teenage boys, teaching the classics in class becomes 'the art of the possible'. There is plenty of interesting stuff, old and new, on the syllabuses but there are certain books that you simply won't touch any more. If I walked into one of my classes at the start of the school year and started dishing out *Vanity Fair*, the male half of the room would take one look and be in uproar. And since the main A-level and GCSE exam boards make no allowance whatsoever for degrees of difficulty, the temptation to teachers is always to dumb down and opt for the simpler and shorter novel.

How many GCSE classes in schools up and down the country are currently studying *The Old Man and the Sea* or *Of Mice and Men*? These are great books, which contain powerful moral messages and will give teenagers – particularly that perverse audience of boys – plenty to think about. But the key fact about both books is that they are 80 pages long and can be studied in bite-size chunks in a matter of a few weeks. The exam boards must take some blame here, as there is no incentive whatsoever to study more challenging works because: (a) the teenagers will be more likely to switch off and give you a harder time teaching the books and (b) their exam grades won't be any better – quite the contrary.

When I taught at an independent school recently, I switched from *The Mayor of Casterbridge* to *Of Mice and Men* as the main English Literature GCSE text, because the Hardy book was proving too demanding. This is despite the fact that I have a doctorate on Hardy and am in a good position to try and spark enthusiasm. The reason for switching texts was length, pure and simple. There was no conception amongst those teenagers of reading ahead, re-reading, or even of reading the book in the first place. They couldn't cope with the idea of a 400-page Victorian classic. Not only is *Of Mice and Men* on user-friendly subjects like 'buddies' (rather than impenetrable subjects like wife-selling) but an invaluable teaching aid comes with it: that excellent 1992 John Malkovich film version.

Given the mounting pressure on teachers to deliver better results, with more and more A grades and A*s being demanded, I was acting sensibly in such a clear case of deliberate dumbing down (though I still feel guilty). The simple fact is that Hardy will never be a hit with teenage boys. *Of Mice and Men*, with its 80 pages and sexy film version, at least has a sporting chance.

But at younger and more mature ages, the picture is much more promising. Pre-teens will continue to plough through all 700 pages of Potter; and yes, bright, enquiring university candidates will continue to pick up a 600-page Monica Ali text. The release of the *Narnia* films too brings a whole new range of beautifully written books into the minds of younger children. My eight-year-old son used to scoff at the idea of reading books. Once he saw the trailer of the first *Narnia* film, he was hooked and couldn't wait to get hold of a copy.

So here, with due deference to the QCA, is my five-point plan for promoting reading, aimed at concerned English teachers and parents alike:

1) Start them young and choose the right book. Be prepared to sit down with all the children in a class and discuss the kinds of book they might like to read on an individual basis: detective, fantasy, comic, classic, travel…

2) Have a broad list of recommended books, with 'something-for-everyone' on it, old and new. Issue a regularly updated reading-list for all age-groups, with realistic choices. Such lists should outline the plot briefly, so that kids know what they're getting in advance.

3) Don't forget to promote poetry. Children of all ages still love to read, write and recite poetry and there is some excellent stuff about, new and old. Perhaps we need to have more poetry-writing competitions aimed at children. Perhaps, too, schools should be more prepared to stage old-style Verse Speaking Competitions. Kids of all ages still seem to enjoy them – I adjudicated one only last month. This whole province of poetry reciting seems to have been taken over by the LAMDA lobby, which is a pity. It's as if poetry isn't part of mainstream education any more.

4) Talk with the child about how the book is going. If they genuinely don't like it, encourage them to try another. Making them persevere with a book they won't enjoy is guaranteed to kill any interest.

5) Award book tokens as presents and prizes.

It's worth re-affirming what would be lost if Hardy and Eliot were not read, or D. H. Lawrence, Virginia Woolf and Henry James. Classic literature transcends its time and is relevant to all ages, all backgrounds, all people. Many classics celebrate the work and achievements of ordinary people. Think of Defoe's Moll Flanders, Hardy's Tess or Thackeray's Becky Sharpe (the original Posh Spice) – when well taught, they should seem relevant, even to today's jaded palates. Traditional literature also happens to be the one art form at which the British Isles has excelled. English Literature has an unparalleled tradition as a quality 'product', one that caters for all likes and dislikes, and the success of Pullman, Rowling *et al.* demonstrates that the art of writing classics-in-the-making continues to be in rude health. It would be a pity if such a rich heritage were not available to future generations. Next time a student tells me he's burnt a copy of The Great Jane, perhaps I'd better smile in pity at him, rather than look so shocked.

Just Stubborn!

Helen Tookey talks with Ed Kirk

You were up reading last night till four o'clock, so I think we can safely say you like reading. How would you rank reading books among other things that you like doing?
Mostly what I do is listen to music and go out with my friends, go to football matches and stuff; so I read when I can't do any of the others. You can read any time, but other things happen at certain times.

This QCA report raises the issue of whether things like texting, and people reading stuff off the internet, in short bits, are having an effect on teenagers' ability to read books, to read long things continuously. Do you think there's any evidence for that?
I don't see how that can make any difference. Reading things off the internet can only make things better; rather than playing a silly game on the internet, if you're actually reading, however short it is, you're still reading.

You don't find it difficult to read long books?
No.

What about your friends? Do they read for pleasure?
It's quite varied. A few of my friends read to find out information, like *A Short History of Nearly Everything* [by Bill Bryson], to find out about things they're interested in. And then a couple of my friends – mainly girls – just read all sorts of stuff, novels about moral issues.

Do you think there's a gender difference?
Well, a little bit, though it's probably more class than gender, because they're my posh friends [laughs]… There's those two, and then the boy who reads most of the time is also quite middle-class.

So do you think growing up in a house with lots of books is more important?
Yes. It's easier to get started.

Does school even that out?

To some extent, the things school gets you to read are things everyone has to read, so you can talk about them. But usually – well, if you're forced to read a book, you don't intend to enjoy it.

You deliberately set out not to like it, because you're being made to read it?
Yeah. Like if my mum gets me books and says they're really good, sometimes I don't read them. I prefer to get my own books, or just random ones people give me. I like choosing for myself. I'm just stubborn!

What did you have to read for GCSE?
Great Expectations, *Romeo and Juliet*, and some poems.

Right. And did everybody read *Great Expectations*?
No. Well, we read the first part of it all together, went through the bits which the exam questions were going to be based on, which was the relationship between the boy and the convict in the beginning; and then we watched the film all the way through, and then we were told to go over the bit we'd done, and read the rest. And I – well, I'd already read it, but I re-read it, and a few of my friends read it.

But a lot of other people didn't?
Yes. I'd say, in a class of 30, probably about 10 read it all. And we were asked to do a synopsis for every chapter, and a lot of people just got them off the internet. I found a lot of them off the internet too just because when I had the homework, that wasn't when I was reading the book.

So you'd read it yourself for enjoyment, and then in school you had to do a completely different thing?
Yes. Because when you're reading something to have fun, it's different from reading something to analyse it, and you don't get half as much enjoyment if you're having to think about every other sentence, rather than just taking it in and subconsciously understanding.

Yes – and knowing that you're being made to read it with certain questions in mind. That could be putting people off.
At school it's a whole different idea about it – it's just you have to read it. Obviously there isn't a choice because that's what you have to do for your GCSE, but there's no extra reading: the teacher doesn't say 'Well, you could read this' or whatever, for further information, it's simply 'You have to read this'.

Do you think the teachers could present things to you in a different way, that would send you off in different directions; or do you think that just wouldn't work anyway; if the teacher says 'Try this', you won't do it?
I think it would work for people who are enthusiastic. Unless you're enthusiastic, it just won't work. If you're going to be stubborn, you're going to be stubborn. But for people who are actually reasonably interested, you could try and feed it by giving them things to look at. We were also doing short stories and I wasn't interested in that at all, I found them quite dull… novels are easier because you find out so much information, they're far more interesting than a short story. It's easier to grow into and actually feel for the characters if you know there's 500 pages' worth rather than 10 pages.

What do you think is the best book you've ever read?
Probably *How it Works*, by Graham Marks. It's about a boy who's not doing very well at college and is just about to fail everything; he just gives up and goes off, doesn't go to college, skives school, and gets into all sorts of trouble and ends up on the streets where he's beaten up. And then he gets his life saved by this person, and then for the rest of the book he's trying to find out who this person is and why they did it. And you get very attached to him. In the end you find out he's sort of an angel, this person. You get more and more clues, but when you find out for real it just sort of hits you, the shock. And no other book's done that – you can tell what's going to happen. So even though you're getting the clues, it's like, oh, wow.

That sounds really good. So next year you're hoping to do English Literature A-level. What are you hoping to get out of that? Why did you choose English at A-level?
I wanted to do Literature because I like reading books. Although it's different when you have to analyse – sometimes not as much fun – it's still interesting to look into why an author has done something. And so I think when I find out what books we're doing, I'll probably read them beforehand, and then I'll find it easier to go over them again and analyse it all, because I'll know what's going on, and I'll have some of my own ideas rather than suddenly jumping in and just starting to look at exactly what's happening before you know everything.

Excellent. Well, thank you very much for your time!

'4Cs' and Could Do Better

Shelley Bridson

So here we were, Jane Davis and I, on a train bound for London with a seminar to attend. The agenda on the table before us was scanned for clues and the potential clashes that might arise in a discussion that was to cover enough questions to fill the lifespan of any passionate reader. What constitutes English Literary Heritage? Where do the classic texts fit in? And what about diversity?

I ought to tell you that our seminar was chaired by Gail Rebuck of Random House, and the discussion was to form part of the consultation process for the Qualifications and Curriculum Authority's deliberations about the future of literary studies in our schools. The QCA's Sue Horner had provided a briefing document, and as we settled into the journey and our old friendship, there was much to occupy our thoughts. The '4Cs', which are to form the underpinning of the future study of English, seem reasonable enough: we wouldn't argue with competence, creativity, or critical skills, but we might have to think through the implications of the 'cultural understanding' aspect. Are we talking about English Literature or English Literatures? Is it English literature if it is translated from another language? And are there any omissions from the '4Cs'? I could think of at least one other that is, in my opinion, crucial.

But our main concern centred upon the question of enthusiasm, even passion. How do we ensure that children get out of the other end of the examination machine with their love of literature intact, or, better, enhanced? The potential negative consequence of an exam-focused approach is that we rob them of one of life's most enriching pleasures. So how might we promote children's entitlement to a wide range of texts, including those that are perceived as difficult, without turning them away? And if, in the interests of accessibility, we deprive them of difficulty, do we thereby deprive them of a sense of mastery and competence? Jane's experience of The Reader's Get Into Reading project seemed relevant here, demonstrating, as it does, that people who missed out at school, residents in the local YMCA, for example, are still able to be guided towards Shakespeare, given the opportunity.

It was in a state of great excitement that we arrived at Random

House, heads full of questions, fearing disappointment, hoping for something good. Sue Horner set out the context for our discussion. The requirements for secondary English education are under revision, with a proposal due in the summer. Once there have been the inevitable adjustments, the rest of the year will be spent looking at GCSE and A-Level. The need to examine the impact of new technologies was touched upon, and we were reminded that teachers have two to three hours per week for 36 weeks of the year in which to cover various kinds of reading and writing and grammar. Teachers perhaps need help in making good choices, in being ambitious for their pupils, in nurturing their enthusiasm and encapsulating the entitlement of children in school to literary texts of high quality.

The first speaker, John Mullan, raised questions about the canon, primarily asking whether it changes over time, by expanding, for example, the central core of what is taught and valued. Echoing Sue Horner, he acknowledged the pressure of time on the syllabus, which sharpens the necessity of reading what is good, as there is no time to waste upon mediocrity. Is relevance what makes things important, or should we be concentrating upon reading the writing, which puts the language at the heart of the matter? If we expand the range of what is available, in order to broaden it, there is the risk of sacrificing depth. Some of those present were most uncomfortable to hear that children often do not read the whole of a novel, and feared that the anthologised approach would end in superficiality. Add to these concerns the question of whether 1914 can still be seen as the birth of the modern, and whether there is any dialogue between the present and the past (T. S. Eliot answers this one) and you have the flavour of this opening section of the discussion.

What part, I wondered, does story play in all this? One of the things that makes us human is our urge to tell and hear stories. Is 'storiness' the thing that links everything? Close reading of the text need not exclude story, as there are ways of getting story into the classroom. Children could write their own stories and read them aloud. After all, literature is about pleasure. If it is taught to the exam, it becomes something other than enjoyable; rather, it is just another goal-oriented activity. We all had stories to share concerning young family members terrified to read around the prescribed texts for fear of missing the ticks in the boxes. It was disturbing to acknowledge that in secondary schools, the pupils have switched off by Year 9, and all the enthusiasm they brought from primary school evaporates. So it becomes a pressing matter to address whether we can bring back the excitement to the classroom. One way of doing this might be through encouraging collaborative reading. As Peggy

Reynolds pointed out, we cannot share the experience in a text, but we can share the experience of reading a text, which is a pleasure.

At this point, we started to feel excited, thinking of ways to improve children's experience of reading. Why not hold literary festivals in schools? Or form reading groups, text-based, to develop the appetite for critical discussion? Such texts need not be for examination. We pondered the reasons for the success of reading groups, and one among us posited the notion that it is, perhaps, a consequence of a broader decline in solitary pursuits. Poetry, as one of us recalled, remains important as a means of fortifying our innerness. How about challenging our children to an exercise in imitation, so that they have the experience of the discipline of writing as the poet did? Would it be possible to allow for pupils to choose a text of their own as part of the syllabus? Then there was much enthusiasm for the return of the unseen practical criticism as an element of the exam. After all, our pupils should have developed the capacity for critical thinking and a vocabulary to facilitate this by the end of the course.

Two more factors seemed important. First, teacher competence and inspiration were considered to be crucially important, although there were two camps as to how many mediocre teachers there might be. Secondly, children need to develop confidence to have an opinion founded on sound critical thinking, so that their sense of entitlement to the heritage is secured. Confidence could well be a fifth C to add to the list. For my own part, I felt that an appropriate C to add would be concentration, which is as essential to reading and writing as to any other discipline. This is not to be developed by dipping into a broad range of anthologised writing: real appreciation demands attention, hence my support for the fewer-texts-more-depth approach, and the emphasis on close reading in groups.

The major challenge facing educators is to make exams consistent with our real intentions for the study of literature. We were asked to write a sentence each about what those intentions should be. These have now been collated and circulated amongst us, and I am heartened to report that words such as enthusiasm, pleasure, love, enjoyment, difficult, connection, challenge and life were evident in the responses.

> All other things to their destruction draw,
> Only our love hath no decay;
> This no tomorrow hath, nor yesterday
>
> John Donne, 'The Anniversary'

Physical and Lavish

Carol Rumens, *Poems 1968–2004*
Bloodaxe, 2004
472 pp, £12

Brian Nellist

Remembering the pianist Phyllis Robinson in a poem published in 2002, Carol Rumens recalls the performance of one of Debussy's *Préludes* in 1958, 'Your technique so physical, so lavish, / I'd call it now, *l'écriture féminine* / For pianists' ('The Submerged Cathedral'). That 'now' is significant because this whole volume expresses the evolution of a single life through a series of exactly contoured moments though, as here, it touches generously on so many others. To be personal for a moment, years ago, before I retired and teaching a close-reading course I was looking for a contemporary poem beyond the usual suspects in my all-too-familiar gallery, picked up the Penguin anthology *Contemporary British Poetry* and found 'A Poem for Chessmen', funny, serious in its observation that tournaments are characteristically male yet centre on the activity of the queen, personal in feeling and recognisably real. Of course I should have been ashamed not to have come across Carol Rumen's name before except that, if you teach literature, the pleasures of the new get lost amidst the competing voices of the past. Anyway the point is that that particular poem does not appear in *Poems 1968–2004*, so maybe I chose badly. Though I suspect there is another reason to do with that adjective 'lavish'.

It is not a word you can use for all poets. Some aim for a crystalline purity and the force given by economy; every line tells, each word counts, all the poems, usually few in number, achieve absolute distinctness, aspire to a discrete memorability. The poems in this volume demand to be read differently from that; collectively they have the fluidity, the constantly shifting, developing form of a single long poem – expressions of a lifetime, active, passionate, above all observant, in love with the world itself and also quarelling with it. If some things drop out of the record like that chess poem, that is part of the abounding generosity of the work, which has a fullness that is even able to spare bits of itself. They used to say that Lawrence, half an hour after arriving in a place, would be discovered excitedly writing his impressions of it, and there is a similar immediacy of response here to so many places, Mexico, Germany, Russia, Northern Ireland, Scotland, Wales and, constantly, the journey back to London, familiar and suburban rather than grandly metropolitan. You could recover a sense of what has been happening to the world in the last forty years from a reading of this volume but all rendered from within a very distinct mind and experience, a woman with her senses, mind and feelings acutely engaged. Here, for example, is a rainbow over Belfast in the poem that gave the title to the 1995 volume, *Best China Sky*:

> A primrose crane, a slope of ochre stacks,
> Stencilled on tissue-thin
> Blue, and, flung between
> These worlds, a sword-flash rainbow,
> The cloud it lies against,
> Metallic as its topmost skin,
> And, round the eyes of hills,
> The tender bluish-green
> That quickly yellows.
>
> The prism comes and goes:
> Wonderful stain, transparency of art!
> A smoke-wraith sails right through it.
> But now it strengthens, glows and braves its span,
> You'd think it was the rim
> Of some resplendent turquoise plate,
> Offering hills and cranes and streets and us
> Fancies designed to melt
> As our fingers touched them.

The accuracy of the eye, the painterly feel for colour, the tactile sense, the individuality of feeling take precedence over any transient political comment. Belfast becomes as enchanted a place as any willow-pattern plate yet the emblem of peace remains indeed as fragile as 'best china'.

George Eliot thought imagination 'a keen consciousness of what *is* and carries the store of definite knowledge as material for the construction of its inward visions'. These poems have that particular quality of imagination. In an earlier poem, 'In Pear Tree Road', the father regrets that the 'white orchards' have been replaced by suburban plane trees but the child loves what is there, the autumn leaves:

> Hanging tight until
> That final crimsoning
> When the small sun had pressed
> A flame hand to each skin.

How precise is that 'small' to describe the wintering sun which still behaves as though it is blistering summer, burning skins, which is exactly the texture of tough plane leaves. Be grateful for a poetry that so respects the substance of things yet remains so intensely personal. A recent poem, 'The Baltic Swan', is one of the best and most sustained expressions I know of the encounter between the human and another sentient creature.

There is always something mysterious about entering another person's life with the kind of intimacy that poetry involves; allusions sometimes remain private though that occasional obscurity only confirms the reality of meeting a real person. In 'The Close Reader' the I becomes a cat-burglar intruding on private property and disturbed by the sudden noise of the householder, heard 'harsh and playful from the drive'. Yet there are no exclusions or reservations in this poetry. It is most definitely '*écriture féminine*' in its physicality, the priority of the body and its reactions, and, I think, its refusal to waste time on resentment. In 'Lines' for example two apparently separated former lovers reunited in a café suddenly become alive to each other again:

> How often, quivering between mind and gland,
> imagination seems no more than the thread
> from a child's hunger-wet mouth to his playful hand,
> frail as the caterpillar's shaken guy-rope –
>   yet this is what tugs and saves us
>   as we climb; this is time's hope.

The whole poem climbs up all the way from accident to intention, from the minimal realism of our lives as a compound of mind and glands to reimagining a new route up the North Face of time. The lines of the poem become literally a life-line negotiated between those physical details of the string of saliva hanging from the mouth of a hungry child and the gossamers of tiny drifting caterpillars.

That verbal vivacity indulges no self-conscious cleverness with words but is the fruit of the intensity with which one woman has lived through her wide range of experience. This is a life-story in poems, expansive, varied yet unified by a single engaging personality. We are not in fantasy-land but a recognisable place with parents and grandparents, the uncle who never grew beyond boyhood, a marriage and children, a separation, lovers, people from all over the place, in Mexico with its alien myths, the countries of what used to be the Soviet bloc, all vividly present, even to the closely observed death of a woman who I take to be the poet's mother, and whose death is being explained to her grandchild. The butterfly is anciently the symbol of the soul in its flight but 'The Storm Butterfly' gazes intently at what we can physically see, the body in its last gasp:

> How can we say what happened? What we saw
> Is all that can be said.
> We can wish, of course, so fiercely
> We nearly pray: that the body forgot to feel
> How hard breath was, that the grace of all it had loved
> Was received in every cell.
> But for you and me, the end
> Of the story is still guesswork,
> And it's only my search for a not-unhappy full-stop
> If I say how it seemed:
> That something slipped very quietly
> And unhesitatingly over
>
> The edge of the day. It didn't
> Flutter, fan itself up
> To the lapis gates, the open halls of nectar
> But fell like a stone, a fruit-stone, newly folded
> To re-unfold, its contract with the earth
> Binding as that of the sky-winged butterfly,
> And death, no less than flight,
> A natural miracle.

The courage in trying to attain a language of consolation without an appeal to religion, though its absence shadows the words here, is not less remarkable than the way the lines seem almost naturally to obey the desire to cross the abyss of stanza ending and full stops. There is a toughness in the wit which gives endurance to this, largely, later poetry that I have quoted:

> Poetry's for grownups. So gather round, who know
> Their music isn't the new rock'n'roll
> But a late quartet that sometimes bursts out laughing.

Long may this voice keep singing its truthful, funny, vigorous, moving song.

> “When thou sigh'st thou sigh'st not wind
> But sigh'st my soul away,
> When thou weep'st, unkindly kind,
> My life's blood doth decay.”
>
> John Donne, 'Song'

Out-of-Place Joy

Russian Short Stories from Pushkin to Buida,
edited by Robert Chandler
Penguin Books Ltd, 2005
ISBN 0140448462

Frances Macmillan

Having read little Russian literature beyond Tolstoy's *Anna Karenina* and *War and Peace*, for which I feel a keen, voracious enjoyment, I was eager to read this collection of short stories. It seemed the ideal introductory package, samples of the best (and most intimidating) Russian writers which could be read in my thirty-minute journeys to and from work every day. I was looking for another Tolstoy, or to be more exact, looking for the sense of deep recognition that I experienced when reading Tolstoy's novels – his magnificently human-hearted honesty about the way people work. Reading this collection of short stories became therefore a little like searching for a familiar face in a bustling train station full of strangers, and I'll confess I struggled with the taut cynicism of Pushkin's fable 'The Queen of Spades', and the surreal weirdness of Dostoevsky's 'Bobok'. There were stories I enjoyed ('In Paris' by Ivan Bunin, 'The Embroidered Towel' by Bulgakov, to name a couple) but I did not find quite what I was looking for.

Two stories by Andrey Platonovich Platonov, appearing three quarters of the way through the collection, took me by surprise. 'The Third Son' is a simply told story of six brothers who are called home to attend their mother's funeral. This is followed by 'The Return', in which a soldier returns to his family after long years away at war. At first the style of writing seemed almost childish; sometimes crude and oddly formal in its straightforwardness, sometimes giddily running on as if the feelings expressed might overflow at any minute. Both stories are about adjustment; the characters try to carve out a new shape for themselves in lives that seem to have displaced them. This displacement results from the most ordinary, and at the same time *extra*ordinary, events, death or homecoming, and occurs painfully in families where mutual ties should be strongest and where roles

– father, brother, son, mother – are most clearly defined. The prose style allows thoughts and feelings, simply and truthfully stated, to appear normal or natural, even though often they are incredibly difficult, alien thoughts for these characters to have.

This precarious balance between common and uncommon, clarity and confusion, gives Platonov's stories intense power. The soldier Ivanov returns home and finds he is shy of his wife and children, particularly of his preternaturally mature son Petya; his own home is 'strange and rather hard to understand'. At the same time, Ivanov is struggling with the mundanity of his situation, his heroic homecoming being so quickly subsumed in everyday life:

> Sitting at the table, among his family, Ivanov realised what he had to do. He must get to work as soon as he could – he had to find a job and earn money, and help his wife bring up the children properly; then everything would gradually get better…

'Gradually get better': leaving his family altogether quickly becomes for Ivanov less painful than the slow prosaic process of fitting back into an old, changed life. At the same time, he does not *only* feel alienation and disappointment in this return:

> Ivanov went up to his wife, put his arms round her and stood there with her, not moving away, feeling the forgotten and familiar warmth of someone he loved.

Platonov's uncomplicated details build up to create lives which are, of course, densely complex. In 'The Third Son', the old man stands with his sons around the body of his wife and, alongside sadness, feels a 'secret excitement and out-of-place joy' as he looks at them. This out-of-place pleasure emerges again in the brothers' late-night hilarity, in the sheer enjoyment of being together, even in such circumstances. Life and death rub together so closely in this household, grief spontaneously converts to joy, and then back again, without warning.

The other side of ordinariness crashes in upon the characters and the reader with the same suddenness. In 'The Return' Ivanov decides to leave his home, his wife's minor infidelity providing an excuse to think himself truly displaced. In a confusion of feeling that is somehow too messy to be pure hypocrisy, Ivanov leaves to find the woman he encountered on the journey home, with whom he was himself unfaithful. Sitting at a crossing, Ivanov notices two children running desperately to reach his train before it passes on:

> Ivanov closed his eyes, not wanting to see and feel the pain of the exhausted children now lying on the ground, and then felt a kind of heat in his chest, as if the heart imprisoned and pining within him had been beating long and in vain all his life and had only now beaten its way to freedom… He suddenly recognised everything he had ever known before, but much more precisely and truthfully.

This is Platonov's one poetic stroke – the exhausted children are Petya and Nastya, Ivanov's own, but he, thinking of something else, fails to recognise them until this moment. This is reality appearing like a revelation, as Ivanov has to turn full-circle in order to re-connect with his family; his 'forgotten and familiar' life.

What started as review of a collection of stories has turned, inevitably perhaps, into a wholehearted recommendation of two tales in particular. This richly varied assortment of fiction contains something to suit everyone, and it is worth persevering with it for that shock of recognition which can happen when least expected. One suggestion to finish: skip the introductions which appear before each author's stories, and go back to them after reading the story if you wish to. They are helpful, and full of enlightening information, but no substitute for encountering the writing itself head-on.

"Beauty is mysterious as well as terrible. God and devil are fighting there, and the battlefield is the heart of man."

Dostoevsky, from *The Brothers Karamazov*

Mentioning the War

Sarah Waters, *The Night Watch*
Virago, 2006
ISBN 1844082466

Eileen Pollard

The Night Watch (2006) by Sarah Waters could break a heart of stone. This poignancy is partly due to its structure which puts lives in reverse, starting in 1947 and finishing in 1941. This is devastating because the book introduces 'a handful of characters, all… more or less unhappy, and all with secrets', uses their pasts to explain why they are unhappy and then ends back at the beginning with glimpses of their (soon to be lost) happiness. This dismantling of hope, and the lack of resolution, fit 'the blighted landscape, the austerity, the sense of inertia, the reticence' of the post-war period. The emotional kick is also due to Waters' sense of the reality of her characters. In a recent essay for *The Guardian* she writes:

> I started to feel as though my characters were real people who had lived through these real nights. Soon they felt closer and more vivid than my Victorian protagonists had ever done.

I second that emotion. In *Fingersmith* (2002), Waters' earlier novel, I delighted in the matriarch Mrs Sucksby, in the crook Gentleman, and in the innocent Susan, but those characters were self-conscious caricatures and Waters' tongue-in-cheek style made me laugh not cry. She has distinctly different attitudes to the two periods of her novels. The nineteenth century she describes as 'a stage set… available for playful reinvention'. The 1940s, on the other hand, belong 'to the people who remember living through them' and she feels a responsibility 'to get things right'. This drove her into rigorous pre-writing research. The decision to set *The Night Watch* in London meant she had to investigate suitable occupations for her single women; one of whom, Julia Standing, she gave architect A. S. G. Butler's solitary job of making a survey of wrecked houses. This job suits Julia's personality because she is a writer and complains of 'author's temperament'. Julia is a fascinating character and maddeningly enigmatic.

> 'Is that what this war's about?' asked Julia.
> 'What do you think it's about?'
> 'I think it's about our love of savagery, rather than our love of beauty. I think the spirit that went into the building of St Paul's has shown itself to be thin: it's like gold leaf, and now it's rising, peeling away. If it couldn't keep us from this – from Hitler and Hitlerism, from Jew-hatred, from the bombing of women and children in cities and towns – what use is it? If we have to fight so hard to keep it – if we have to have elderly men patrolling the roofs of churches, to sweep incendiaries from them with little brushes! – how valuable can it be? How much at the centre of the human heart?'
> Helen shivered – impressed, suddenly, by the awful sadness of Julia's words; and glimpsing a sort of darkness in her – a frightening, baffling darkness. She touched her arm.
> 'If I thought like that, Julia,' she said softly, 'I'd want to die.'

This is Julia's longest speech in *The Night Watch* and yet even this leaves much unsaid. I want to know what provokes her feeling – what background, what experiences, what principles – and Waters will not say. The language of her novel is pared down to a sort of laconic off-handedness, which makes *The Night Watch* into a novel of unanswered questions. Does Julia actually love Helen? What is the relationship between Duncan and Mr Mundy? How did Julia meet Kay? This teasing dynamic within Waters' writing marks a departure from her previous novels. In *Fingersmith* it is what is revealed that grabs the reader's attention, but in *The Night Watch* what Waters concedes is not so interesting – her characters' secrets are fairly opaque – but I am fascinated by what she implies. She describes the 1940s as 'a time of bleak passions tucked firmly away behind façades of understatement and good manners' and sees her challenge as the suggestion of 'a depth of feeling behind the apparently lightly placed word'. Interestingly, Waters illustrates the workings of this mechanism explicitly using another conversation between Helen and Julia:

> 'The fact is, Julia, I'm afraid to be drunk while I'm with you.'
> It seemed to [Helen] that there could be no mistaking the meaning of her words: that they had penetrated some

> thin but resilient membrane, made a tear through which a heap of unruly passions would now come tumbling… But Julia laughed again, and must have turned her head, for her breath no longer came against Helen's lips; and when she spoke, she spoke musingly, distantly.

Helen's apparently lightly placed words, 'I'm afraid to be drunk while I'm with you', are a coded declaration of love. But Julia's interpretation of this statement is held back in her musing and distant reply. Waters' narration simultaneously reveals and suppresses characters' thoughts. At this moment of emotional intensity all the reader is given is 'Julia laughed again'.

However, despite the elusiveness of these exchanges, it really is the bleak passions tucked behind the manner that give richness to the whole setting. Waters explains:

> With *The Night Watch*, as with my previous novels, I wanted to focus on characters and stories which felt embedded in their particular historical context, yet told us something slightly new about it… it seemed to me that one way to achieve this might be to focus on the period's lesbian and gay life.

This sounds artificial and agenda'd but essentially *The Night Watch* is about the highs and lows of several love affairs. Aside from politics, *The Night Watch* is simply about love – love as intoxicator, love as burden, love as destroyer – these are its guises not the categories of sexuality. Helen explains: 'It never felt strange, as perhaps it ought to have done… But then, so many impossible things were becoming ordinary, just then.'

My favourite part of *The Night Watch* is the 1947 section with its terrible and tangible post-war paralysis. My only criticism of this novel is oddly one that Waters has levelled herself:

> The brooding turbulent energy of the [post-war] period, however, is something *The Night Watch*, with its retrospective movement, can only really hint at. It's a subject, I'm beginning to suspect, for a whole new novel. And now that I've finally got those bomb stories off my chest, I'm looking forward to exploring it.

I can hardly wait.

Dostoevsky's *Devils*

Rowan Williams

A novel dealing with terrorism, suicide and child abuse sounds uncomfortably contemporary; and so it is. But it is sobering to realise that one of Europe's foremost novelists should have been reflecting on these things as long ago as 1871. Fyodor Dostoevsky was already a major figure in the Russian cultural scene when he published *Devils*, the third of the four great novels of his maturity. By this time, he had returned to Christian faith and practice, and saw himself as called to defend this faith in his writing. But this did not mean that he wrote improving stories on religious subjects. His way of defending Christianity was to try to show how it could cope with the most horrific and extreme of human situations. He never gives easy answers, but expects his readers to face the worst the world can offer so that the scale of God's grace becomes even more astonishing.

By 1871, he was regarded with some suspicion by many who had been friends and admirers in his earlier days. He had dramatically rejected the political radicalism of his youth – though what replaced it was in many ways even more radical. And the publication of *Devils* fulfilled the worst fears of his former allies. It is a merciless exposé of certain aspects of the Russian revolutionary movements of the mid-nineteenth century, and of the various kinds of revolutionary and terrorist psychology. We meet people who are simply confused, who want a better world and who love the ordinary folk of Russia but who have no basis for their commitments and can be exploited by others. We meet the administrative fanatic who is ready to kill huge numbers of the population in order to organise a supposedly fair world and make sure that the right people stay in charge. We meet the lonely visionary who concludes that the only way of showing that he is really free and Godlike is to commit suicide.

But the two central characters in the revolutionary circle are the most disturbing of all. Pyotr Verkhovensky is a brilliant manipulator, whose only real interest is in controlling others. We never learn what he really believes, and in a sense it doesn't matter. He understands group psychology perfectly; he carefully plans the murder of one member of the group, involving all the others so as to bind them closer together (Dostoevsky based this on a real incident of the time). He shows different faces to different people, he makes himself popular with fashionable progressive circles in the town, and at the end simply walks away from all the consequences of what he has done.

But he has one weak spot. He is obsessed with the man who, he believes, has the capacity to be a real leader, Nikolai Stavrogin. Stavrogin attracts all sorts of projections: he is intelligent, wildly independent, mysterious and charismatic, a 'messianic' figure. All around him are people who are fascinated by him and would do anything for him. But increasingly we see that there is nothing behind the façade. He is a desperately empty person, paralysed by his own sense of meaninglessness. He cannot take on any role in Pyotr's conspiracy, nor can he consummate any real relationship. His life has been a series of arbitrary experiments in extreme behaviour to try and force himself to feel that there is a real self there; and it has all failed. He is one of Dostoevsky's most frightening characters.

These two diabolical characters don't come from nowhere. Their parents also figure in the book. Pyotr's father is a vain and silly old man, who loves to think of himself as a daring revolutionary writer; Nikolai's mother is an equally silly woman, caught up in a whole complex of self-deceit. For years she has looked after Pyotr's father (they are both widowed), as if there is a sort of imitation marriage between them, one without either sex or love. The message is clear: the demonic evil of the two younger men comes from this sterile, fantasy-ridden atmosphere, full of large talk about change and progress, but with absolutely no spiritual or moral substance. One generation's flabby fashions become destructive horrors in the next generation. You can see why Dostoevsky's novel was so unpopular with progressives in Russia at the time.

Can there be redemption for people like these, people whose emptiness invites the devil in? Pyotr, as we have seen, walks offstage at the end, unscathed and unchanged; he is the most literally diabolical character because we cannot imagine him developing, acquiring ordinary human emotions. Nikolai is more complex. In the original draft of the novel, Dostoevsky wrote a chapter which he was never allowed to publish because it was thought too shocking; it was only printed in 1921. It shows Nikolai going to visit a retired bishop in a monastery to try to confess to him and find a way out of his private hell. It turns out that what he has to confess is that he has, some time before, seduced a small child, who later committed suicide. The story is told with almost unbearable realism, and makes very painful reading indeed.

What should he do? Should he make a great public confession? The bishop asks whether he is humble enough to accept not only the hatred and the pity but also the mockery that will result from his publishing of his record of all this; and whether he can follow through the consequences and live a truly repentant life. Stavrogin finally leaves in anger; the bishop warns him that he will now find some new atrocity to get involved in, so as to blot out the memory of the story he has just told and to put off confessing it. For a moment a door has opened, but Stavrogin cannot – will not – do anything to accept the possibility of forgiveness.

It is hard now to imagine how people could understand Stavrogin without reading this chapter, because only here do we see the depth of his despair and self-loathing. But after this, it is no surprise that he becomes more and more frozen and dead, and that he finally kills himself.

The surprise is that the one character who does find a kind of redemption is Pyotr's father, Stepan. Shocked and disoriented by the violence that has erupted around him, finally recognising that his situation is without love or honesty, he takes to the road, not knowing what will happen or where he wants to go. Sick and exhausted and beginning to wander in his mind, he meets a travelling Bible-seller, a poor and unassuming woman who doesn't know what he's talking about most of the time, but only knows that she has to tell him what he needs to know. She reads the gospel to him, the story from St Luke of the demoniac possessed by the legion of devils. Through all Stepan's confusion and weakness, he recognises that he has heard something that could change everything. He dies saying that God is necessary after all – because only God can be loved eternally and unconditionally.

It is a bleak and difficult novel – though also a very funny one at times, as Dostoevsky's blackest humour is allowed full rein. What makes it so well worth reading now is its unsparing vision of what destructive forces come into the world when there is a vacuum of spiritual understanding. The end of faith doesn't lead to a calm agnosticism, but to a terrible world where you have no means of knowing truth from lies or even life from death. It tells us that terrorism is a spiritual problem before it is a political one; whatever clothes it dresses up in, religious or national or ideological, what it feeds on is spiritual emptiness. It tells us that liberalism is not enough; there must be a vital and positive commitment to freedom and to mutual responsibility – Dostoevsky's most central insight is about the way we are all responsible for all others. And it tells us that human beings need something to love that is eternal and unchanging; only the utterly consistent love of God can draw out of us the love we are capable of at our most free and creative.

Dostoevsky doesn't produce a bit of easy propaganda but a whole world of complicated interactions designed to show how in the Russia of his day the Christian faith offered the only real hope of change that was free of fantasy and violence and one or another sort of denial of humanity. It is not an argument for God and Christ – that isn't how novels work, and you can appreciate the novel without having to say yes to the vision. But if you want to see how faith can illuminate some of the most dreadful places in modern experience and the modern psyche, this is one of the greatest resources you could have.

The Personal Canon: Why I Like Chekhov And Don't Like O'Connor

Ann Stapleton

> How can you love God whom you do not see, if you do not love your neighbor whom you see, whom you touch, with whom you live?
>
> Mother Teresa of Calcutta

In a letter to I.L. Shtcheglov, the Russian fiction writer and dramatist Anton Chekhov admitted to being terrified of the word 'art': 'I divide all works into two classes: those I like and those I don't. I have no other criterion, and if you ask me why I like Shakespeare and don't like Zlatovratsky, I don't venture to answer.' And thus a breath of fresh air from 1890s' Russia reaches us even here, and returns us post haste to the very reason we read books at all: to like them. Of course, in order to find the ones we love, we must read a fair number of ones we don't. That is the price of admission to the strange worlds in our heads. And as the years pass by and the books pile up, slowly but quite surely we establish a personal canon, based entirely, as it should be, on Chekhov's one criterion: a private notion of what is true and good.

When compiling one's own canon, it is quite as useful to consider who is to be debarred as who will be granted admittance, as I was reminded recently when I happened to be reading, during the same space of time and attention, the stories of Chekhov and those of his companion in pessimism, the American, Southern, religio-goth Flannery O'Connor. Both authors believe that human existence is a disappointing affair at best. Chekhov: 'Life is grey, there are no happy people to be seen.' O'Connor, in a fine bit of understatement: 'The novelist with Christian concerns will find in modern life distortions which are repugnant to him.' Where Chekhov sees a godless universe that has failed its people, O'Connor sees a people who have failed their God. Yet strange how dissimilarly these two peerers into darkness can affect the reader's heart. Though neither is a fan of life on earth, as

Chekhov would say, they are singing in very different operas.

If O'Connor is obsessed with the idea that we are mortal beings who may die at any time, and who therefore need to be urged (forced) to put our spiritual accounts in order (this is her constant, urgent message, and the felt integrity of it pervades her essays), for most of her characters, the crisis comes too late to embrace (in life) the lessons revelation might teach. The grandmother in O'Connor's short story 'A Good Man is Hard to Find,' for example, reaches out in compassion to an escaped convict called the Misfit whose companions are in the process of executing her entire family. 'Why you're one of my babies. You're one of my own children!' she says to him, in a moment of epiphany, whereupon she promptly receives three bullets in the chest for her trouble. O'Connor may teach her characters how to die, but she seems to know little of how they might go on living. The awakenings she imposes on them are so extreme that generally they don't survive them; in these stories, the typical reward for spiritual insight is death: an entire family is annihilated; a woman is gored by a bull; a young boy hangs himself; a man drowns his idiot cousin while baptizing him; a child has her brains bashed out on a rock by her own grandfather.

It is a strange feature of O'Connor's fiction that her well-drawn characters, by and large remarkable for their Old Testament originality and a somehow admirable, entrenched stubbornness that often approaches monomania, come to seem almost interchangeable. But the locus of O'Connor's interest is not to be found in their individuality or uniqueness, or even in their shared humanity. Like the half-mad itinerant preacher in fellow Southerner Eudora Welty's story 'A Still Moment,' O'Connor's authorial voice calls out, 'I must have souls, and souls I must have!' As this rigidity of vision and indifference to earthly striving in all its imperfection leaves no room for my view of the cosmos, I resist the coercion, and resist it mightily. I am reminded of a scene from the seventies' television show *The Waltons* in which the father John, played by Ralph Waite, when asked by his wife to attend a church service presided over by a holy rollerish minister, says, in quiet and dignified refusal, 'I'll not be shouted at, Liv.'

As to O'Connor's 'black comedy' so beloved by academics attracted to her Quentin Tarantino-style stagings of human events (who mistake the chaff blown in their faces for the intended wheat, and thereby misapprehend both her technique and her artistic vision), the humor may simply be the result of a reader's version of progressive exposure. This is the counseling technique whereby one conquers a fear (of riding in elevators or highway driving, for example) by repeatedly engaging in the activity until one becomes accustomed to it, and thus inured to the distress it once evoked. When the first O'Connor story you read ends in a macabre death, you are shocked, shocked! By the fourth or fifth such demise, the by now expected gruesome plot twist may elicit only a weary half-smile and a roll of the eyes.

If Eudora Welty, a contemporary of O'Connor and a direct inheritor of Chekhov, has been accused of loving all her characters, O'Connor seems to love none. Her fiction is most notable for an almost total absence of earthly love or joy. These are perhaps the coldest stories in the canon. In O'Connor's 'Revelation,' a woman hosing out a concrete hog pen, 'blindly pointing the stream of water in and out of the eye of the old sow whose outraged squeal she did not hear,' experiences a vision of a 'vast horde of souls' 'rumbling toward heaven.' 'Yet she could see by their shocked and altered faces that even their virtues were being burned away.' And that is the difficulty with O'Connor's fiction, and the reason it will never enter my personal canon: she is so bent on eradicating sin that she burns away all love as well.

Like O'Connor, Chekhov is fundamentally a pessimist who perceives the ordinary human life as being at the mercy of vast, disinterested (and therefore often brutal) forces. Joy in Chekhov almost always goes arm in arm with sorrow, as they push on through the world like an old married couple, attuned even in sleep to one another's rhythms. In Chekhov, love exists, but its small hopes rise and fall on an indifferent ocean of fate, and it is borne along in the frail vessel of the body, that will too soon come ashore at its own extinction. In an early story of his called 'The Huntsman,' the brief happiness of a wife upon meeting her husband in the woods (we learn that they will no longer be living together) diminishes before our eyes as she concentrates fiercely on the image of his white cap disappearing from sight. In 'Oysters,' the dinner given by a crowd to a starving boy is imagined as a frightening fare with eyes, and teeth that bite ('The grown-ups would take it and eat it, eat it alive with its eyes, its teeth, its legs! While it squeaked and tried to bite their lips'); the meal is consumed in a fever, as the father, too timid to beg his own dinner, goes hungry. (When Chekhov died, in Germany, his body went home to Russia on a railroad car used to haul oysters.) The monk Ieronim of 'Easter Eve' must ferry the revelers to and from the spectacular Easter Eve celebration in darkness, while mourning the death of his dearest friend: 'He always used to come to the bank and call to me that I might not be afraid on the ferry. He used to get up from his bed at night on purpose for that. He was a kind soul.'

In one of Chekhov's most moving tales, aptly titled 'Misery,' he describes the plight of Iona, a brokenhearted man who can find no one who will listen to him talk about his son's death:

> His misery is immense, beyond all bounds. If Iona's heart were to burst and his misery to flow out, it would flood the whole world, it seems, but yet it is not seen. It has found a hiding-place in such an insignificant shell that one would not have found it with a candle by daylight.

Finally, failed by all the people around him, the man unburdens himself to his little horse: 'The little mare munches, listens, and breathes on her master's hands. Iona is carried away and tells her all about it.'

Chekhov's subversive response to a world that, according to his observations, is 'a nasty business for everyone' is to communicate that suffering to the reader, so that he may look around his life with new eyes and feel the predicament of his fellow creatures, which is his own predicament as well. In this passage from a letter to Madame M. V. Kiselyov, Chekhov's openheartedness extends even to the birds, though he also makes allusion to the plight of humans in a hostile existence:

> It is devilishly cold, but the poor birds are already flying to Russia! They are driven by homesickness and love for their native land. If poets knew how many millions of birds fall victims to their longing and love for their homes, how many of them freeze on the way, what agonies they endure on getting home in March and at the beginning of April, they would have sung their praises long ago! … Put yourself in the place of a corncrake who does not fly but walks all the way, or of a wild goose who gives himself up to man to escape being frozen… Life is hard in this world!

That we might do better by one another, be kinder, alleviate more suffering, was a constant preoccupation for Chekhov (his writing is its embodiment), who worked ceaselessly, to the detriment of his own precarious health, to improve the lives around him. As a physician ('Medicine is my lawful wife and literature is my mistress'), he provided treatment, and often free medication, to thousands; as a friend, he offered encouragement and sound advice to the locals, who adored him. He contributed 'whole bales of books' to the library in Taganrog, his birthplace, turning it into a first-rate learning institution. He built schools and roads and a fire-station for his village, and even devised a relief fund to buy up the starving horses of indigent peasants so that the animals might be fed through the winter and then returned to their owners in time for the spring planting. He made a harrowing three-thousand-mile journey across Siberia on wretched roads often closed by flooding to reach Sakhalin Island. There he interviewed all ten thousand of the inmates, and his findings helped to achieve significant prison reforms. (Once back home, he sent shipments of books to the prisoners.) And, as described in this passage by his brother Mihail, he battled heroically against the spread of cholera:

> Chekhov as a doctor and a member of the Sanitary Council was asked to take charge of a section. He immediately gave his services for nothing. [...] For several months Chekhov scarcely got out of his chaise. During that time he had to drive all over his section, receive patients at home, and do his literary work. He returned home shattered and exhausted, but always behaved as though he were doing something trivial; he cracked little jokes and made everyone laugh as before, and carried on conversations with his dachshund, Quinine, about her supposed sufferings.

Though these activities imply a belief in humankind, and a conviction that life might be made better by our efforts, Chekhov, whose childhood was a bizarre combination of severe beatings from his father and a deep involvement in church life, did not retain a religious faith into adulthood and wondered at intellectuals who were also believers. At the same time, he had a detailed and first hand knowledge of religious ritual and in his stories accords the faithful a tender respect. If he often felt the world to be, to borrow a line from his play *The Seagull*, 'Cold, cold, cold. Empty, empty, empty. Frightful, frightful, frightful,' at the same time, he understood it to be the only life we have. Therefore, his impulse was not to rob anyone else of his belief, lest it be the only thing standing between him and the extinction of his hope. In the words of critic Leonid Grossman, Chekhov was 'a probing Darwinist with the love of St. Francis of Assisi for every living creature.'

'Gusev,' one of Chekhov's most affecting stories, considers the death from tuberculosis of a man at sea, so far from his home in Russia that he wonders if his family will ever learn of his demise. Traveling home from Sakhalin Island, Chekhov had observed an ocean burial:

> On the way to Singapore we threw two corpses into the sea. When one sees a dead man, wrapped in sailcloth, fly, turning somersaults in the water, and remembers that it is several miles to the bottom, one feels frightened, and for some reason begins to fancy that one will die oneself and will be thrown into the sea.

And it is this heartfelt identification with another life that permits the reader entry into its mystery as well, as if Chekhov's hand holds open the door for us to pass through. This is the very essence of literature's reason for being, the measure of what it can do, and the standard by which lesser talents (such as O'Connor's) must ultimately be judged. Chekhov wrote that his concern was 'to write, not teach! … Living truthful images generate thought, but thought cannot create an image.' Nor can religious conviction substitute for love. Chekhov, who has no god or thought of an afterlife, pities the lives of men on earth, so much less beautiful than those they dream of, and in so doing, he also mourns the lives they will never lead. As Harold Bloom has written, 'the unlived life is the unique obsession of Chekhov,' and all of his work points not only toward what his characters might have experienced if the world were a different sort of place, but also toward the unexpressed pity and solidarity in our own hearts, for which he makes us responsible.

Literally on his last legs, Gusev wants to go topside to escape the stifling cabin, and another patient, a man with his own arm in a sling, observing that Gusev cannot manage this for himself, carries him up to where he can see 'Overhead deep sky, bright stars, peace and stillness, exactly as at home in the village, below darkness and disorder.' The other men are lying asleep on the deck as if enchanted, in Chekhov's vision of the final, communal sleep that awaits all of us.

And then we are given this passage of helpless recognition and deep pessimism about life on earth, which could almost have been written by O'Connor herself:

> The sea has no sense and no pity. If the steamer had been smaller and not made of thick iron, the waves would have crushed it to pieces without the slightest compunction, and would have devoured all the people in it with no distinction of saints or sinners. The steamer had the same cruel and meaningless expression. This monster with its huge beak was dashing onwards, cutting millions of waves in its path; it had no fear of the darkness nor the wind, nor of space, nor of solitude, caring for nothing, and if the ocean had its people, this monster would have crushed them, too, without distinction of saints or sinners.

Yet this terrifying realization, wholly without illusion, somehow moves Chekhov toward, not away from, the small figures who had no part in creating such a disinterested universe, but who nevertheless find themselves at its (lack of) mercy.

'And are you afraid to die?' the soldier asks Gusev. And he answers also for the consumptive Chekhov, who from an early age was the sole support of his much-loved family: 'Yes. I am sorry for the folks at home. […] Everything will go to ruin without me, and father and my old mother will be begging their bread, I shouldn't wonder.' And this statement expresses perfectly the human fears implicit always in the ties of love, for the immensity of the dark waters and the thought of extinction carry with them, too, the opposite fear: that our deaths will matter hardly at all, a little ripple seven days out from land, with, to remember them, only a few other mortals whose lives will also end. The human burden that O'Connor never takes up, but that Chekhov, with his bad lungs and his lion heart, can never bring himself to put down.

Gusev goes back below, where, 'worn out with nightmares, his cough, and the stifling heat, towards morning he [falls] into a sound sleep.' 'He slept for two days, and at midday on the third two sailors came down and carried him out.'

> He was sewn up in sailcloth and to make him heavier they put with him two iron weights. Sewn up in the sailcloth he looked like a carrot or a radish: broad at the head and narrow at the feet. … Before sunset they brought him up to the deck and put him on a plank.

And what the humane Chekhov does here is the essence of his genius. He never tells us Gusev dies! He does not relate what is done to 'the body,' but continues to call the man by his name, throughout the harrowing scene in which poor Gusev (and along with him – think of it – even his ability to imagine the ocean snapping at its chains, or to remember what snow feels like against his cheek) is catapulted into the sea, sinks down and down (as we accompany him!), until a shark finds him and rips open even the sailcloth, his only remaining bit of protection (really only a kindness to the eyes of the men who must watch him disappear into the waves). During all this, he is still Gusev, so painfully precious to us, and irreplaceable, because he is precious to his creator. And when our eyes finally turn away from the body to follow the iron weight down to the bottom, it is our own death we are watching, our own life we mourn. For a few brief moments, all distance between character and reader is erased, and we are Gusev.

When we finish reading Chekhov, the skeptic, and turn back to the world, we feel an almost fearful new tenderness toward the human beings around us. We look anew – with wonder at their uniqueness, with pity for their sorrow and loneliness, with pride in their against-all-odds endurance. They look so beautiful to us that we can hardly stand it. And so we go out searching for the heartbroken little man with the horse – where can he be but everywhere we go? We want to say to him, as O'Connor forgets to say to her God, 'Tell me about your son. What was he like? You must love him very much.' For God so LOVED the world is how the verse goes. For the greatest of these is – no, not faith, but love. Strange that the spirit at the very heart of Christianity (like Chekhov's stories, accessible not only to the faithful, but also to secularists like me – in fact, to anyone human) should be made starkly visible in tales of ordinary human suffering told by an avowed skeptic, someone it does not seem quite accurate to call a nonbeliever.

In 'Gusev,' a boat passes by in which Chinamen, peddling their wares, hold up caged canaries in dazzling sunlight, and call out, 'It sings!,' Chekhov's stunning dual image both of the human soul, a persistent small brightness glimpsed imperfectly through its little crate of bones, and also of the world's ungraspable beauty, moving past us so swiftly that we can scarcely apprehend it, that both assaults us with our own longing and consoles us even to the end of life. I greedily hoard this, in astonishment and sorrow, for my canon that I hope will somehow outlive me. And is it Chekhov's voice or my own?, and are we talking to each other, or to Gusev? I'm not sure, two agnostics watching the light on the sea, the 'tender, joyous, passionate colours for which it is hard to find a name in human speech,' and in confusion and wonder approaching at the same time, from above ground and below, this most human of Christian thoughts: 'I made a covenant with you, and you became mine.'

> Men reject their prophets and slay them, but they love their martyrs and honour those whom they have slain.
>
> Dostoevsky, from *The Brothers Karamazov*

Strange Cold World

Donna Tartt, *The Secret History*
Penguin, 1992

Helen Tookey

The back-cover blurb describes *The Secret History* as a murder mystery, but this is a somewhat slant description, since we are told on the first page of the book's Prologue who has been killed and who has done the killing. The mystery, which the first 300 pages of the novel (Book I) wind around and gradually reveal both to us and to the narrator, is *why* the murder has to take place. The second half of the book depicts, in minutely observed detail, the consequent outworkings of guilt, as the characters fall apart under the pressure of their (undiscovered) crime. If this sounds familiar, it is, to some extent: *The Secret History* could be described as *Crime and Punishment* relocated in time and space to a New England college campus at some indeterminate point in the 1970s. Tartt's characters share with Dostoyevsky's Raskolnikov a philosophical commitment to escaping the constraints of 'civilisation'; in both books, the murders are the result of a deliberate intellectual attempt to step beyond the ordinary mores of society and human relationships. And in both cases, the characters discover that this is not so easy to do.

Crime and Punishment is a shadowy presence within the book, erupting once – with startling effect – in a direct quotation. But Tartt's novel also stands by itself as a compelling, disturbing, beautifully written and even darkly funny book. Our narrator is Richard Papen, a nineteen-year-old from Plano, an ugly 'silicon village' in northern California. Richard introduces his story as follows:

> Does such a thing as 'the fatal flaw', that showy dark crack running down the middle of a life, exist outside literature? I used to think it didn't. Now I think it does. And I think that mine is this: a morbid longing for the picturesque at all costs.

In search of the picturesque, Richard scrambles his way onto an English literature degree course at Hampden College in Vermont.

The early part of the book is suffused with the atmosphere of autumn in New England, as seen for the first time through the eyes of a Californian:

> Trees creaking with apples, fallen apples red on the grass beneath, the heavy sweet smell of them rotting on the ground and the steady thrumming of wasps around them. Commons clock tower: ivied brick, white spire, spellbound in the hazy distance. The shock of first seeing a birch tree at night, rising up in the dark as cool and slim as a ghost. And the nights, bigger than imagining: black and gusty and enormous, disordered and wild with stars.

Richard's fascination with the picturesque goes into overdrive when he tries to sign up for classes in ancient Greek ('the only language in which I was at all proficient') and discovers that the tutor, an enigmatic loner named Julian Morrow, will take only a small number of hand-picked students; and when he observes these students, four boys and a girl, it becomes imperative to Richard that he join them, become like them, become one of them:

> [Julian's] students – if they were any mark of his tutelage – were imposing enough, and different as they all were they shared a certain coolness, a cruel, mannered charm which was not modern in the least but had a strange cold breath of the ancient world: they were such magnificent creatures, such eyes, such hands, such looks – *sic oculos, sic ille manus, sic ora ferebat*. I envied them, and found them attractive; moreover this strange quality, far from being natural, gave every indication of having been intensely cultivated… Studied or not, I wanted to be like them.

Much later, after the murder, Richard reflects on the twisted way in which this wish has come true: 'Now it made me sick, knowing there was no way out. I was stuck with them, with all of them, for good.'

Accepted into Julian's classes, Richard begins to live between two worlds – both of which are brilliantly and richly depicted by Tartt. There is the present-day world of college life, a world of crystal meth, acid and booze, of basement parties and Judy Poovey, the good-hearted gossip queen down the hall; and there is the 'strange cold' world of the ancient Greeks and their language, the world of Julian Morrow and his students: terrifying and cerebral Henry, nervy aesthete Francis, the beautiful twins Charles and Camilla, manipulative but naive Bunny, and the outsider, Richard. Of these two worlds it is the college world, with its drugs and scams and petty crime, that will turn out to be the innocent one, the world that Richard will lose forever ('I was struck by a horrible thought: *Is this what it's like? Is this the way it's going to be from now on?*'). In one of his classes Julian describes the 'terrible seduction' of Dionysiac ritual and its place in the Greek worldview:

> 'Do you remember what we were speaking of earlier, of how bloody, terrible things are sometimes the most beautiful? It's a very Greek idea, and a very profound one. Beauty is terror. Whatever we call beautiful, we quiver before it. And what could be more terrifying and beautiful, to souls like the Greeks or our own, than to lose control completely? To throw off the chains of being for an instant, to shatter the accident of our mortal selves?'

It is Henry, Francis and the twins' attempt to achieve this escape from normal being, to experience the self-shattering mystery of the Greek rituals, that leads, first to a possibly accidental killing, and then to the quite deliberate murder of Bunny, in a chain of events seemingly as inexorable as the patterns of the Greek language itself. 'How can I make you see it,' muses Richard,

> this strange harsh light which pervades Homer's landscapes and illumines the dialogues of Plato, an alien light, inarticulable in our common tongue? Our shared language is a language of the intricate, the peculiar, the home of pumpkins and ragamuffins and bodkins and beer, the tongue of Ahab and Falstaff and Mrs Gamp; and while I find it entirely suitable for reflections such as these, it fails me utterly when I attempt to describe in it what I love about Greek, that language innocent of all quirks and cranks; a language obsessed with action, and with the joy of seeing action multiply from action, action marching relentlessly ahead and with yet more actions filing in from either side to fall into neat step at the rear, in a long straight rank of cause and effect toward what will be inevitable, the only possible end.

This book brilliantly charts such a sequence of cause and effect, from Richard's 'morbid longing' to Bunny's death and its consequences. Tartt's achievement is to create a completely realised world peopled with compelling characters. We are drawn to Henry's cold Greek world as well as appalled by its consequences; we feel ourselves, with Richard, enclosed in a narrowing world of guilt and fear: *It was I killed the old pawnbroker woman and her sister Lizaveta with an axe.* As Richard tells us at the very beginning,

I suppose at one time in my life I might have had any number of stories to tell, but now there is no other. This is the only story I will ever be able to tell.

Outrageous Nonsense

Nicolai Gogol, 'The Nose'
translation by Ronald Wilks
Penguin

Andrew Mellor

Years ago at university a housemate asked me, probably over a pan of slowly warming spaghetti hoops, if I had ever read Gogol's story about 'a pompous bureaucrat hurrying around St Petersburg in search of his own nose'. Thinking of that question always made me chuckle but I avoided getting hold of a copy of the story to read for some years. I suppose my friend's summary seemed so amusing in itself that I was reluctant to confuse it with a genuine piece of literature which would supplant his hilarious description.

It was a couple of years later that I heard someone else, probably a Radio 3 commentator, utter a similar cadence, this time, 'the opera by Shostakovich, which tells the story of a haughty bureaucrat hastily chasing his own nose around the city of St Petersburg'. Now it was time to read Gogol's 'The Nose' (which Shostakovich later scored as an opera); the self-contained one-liner from my erstwhile housemate had been disfigured. I've not heard the opera by Shostakovich – one of those pieces that I've not come across – but even so, reading Gogol's story, my mind fills with musical gestures from Shostakovich symphonies, concertos and film scores that tickle and terrify me as much as Gogol's bizarre scenarios and childlike turns of phrase.

If it's not too much of a generalisation, there's something about Russian art (particularly in Gogol and Shostakovich, it seems to me), which even at the very depths of despair is close to a raucous humour. Shostakovich's symphonies frequently lunge from the most terrifying to a most preposterous parody in seconds, sometimes simultaneously conveying both states, creating a nightmarish soundscape in which even the most amiable of tunes can turn on you. In the symphonies which are predominantly weighty and brooding, twists and schizophrenic themes lead to a feeling of insecurity which Shostakovich must have known very well as an artist under Stalin. Celebrations are often short-lived, crushed by inevitable proletarian dictates – dictates which Shostakovich often renders with a twisted parody rather than a righteous sermon. A similarly keen wit and ability to adjust the context are found in 'The Nose'. In the dreamlike world encountered in Gogol's story, it is impossible to know whether what you are reading is meant as reality, dream or satire. Neither as Gogol begins each new episode in his story can you detect the moment at which you drift from one realm into another. At what point does a clarinet melody by Shostakovich transform from an ordered almost neo-classical 'tune' into a deranged, mocking and savage siren? It's almost impossible to say, and moreover the result is not a fractured, two-part theme, but a single, idiosyncratic musical gesture.

In 'The Nose', the disconcerting feeling of a clash between mundane reality and total fantasy is seasoned with a gift for language and irony that seems uncannily contemporary. As a reader, you find yourself questioning your own understanding of reality as, at the crux of the story, the human beings – in whom you might, at first, have placed belief – begin to be 'supernaturalised' by Gogol. It's one thing empathising with the civil servant Major Kovalyov when he loses his nose but what are we to make of the occasion when he accosts the renegade nose in a public building and speaks to it as if it were a citizen of St Petersburg?

> [Kovalyov] turned around to tell the nose in uniform straight out that it was only masquerading as a state councillor, that it was an impostor and a scoundrel, and really nothing else than his own private property, *his* nose... But the nose had already gone: it had managed to slip off unseen, probably to pay somebody a visit.

This cast-off from the narrator, 'probably to pay somebody a visit', has echoes of my housemate's original comment. It seems so fresh, so citric, and utterly suggestive of all sorts of ideas. Why, most importantly, has the one assumed bedrock of sanity, the narrator, suddenly revealed a disconcerting sympathy with the most absurdly unreal element of the story?

It's precisely this blindness to the absurdity of the unfolding plot that gives the story its satirical weight. Whatever commentators pinpoint as the interpretations intended by Gogol, perhaps the most obvious (not necessarily the most important) is his reflection of a society too obsessed with procedure to detect the blatantly unreal. Gogol probably had it a little easier than Shostakovich in terms of state intervention and censorship of his works – when you compare the Russian political climate of his 1830s' St Petersburg with Shostakovich's 1930s' Leningrad. But that doesn't make his commentary less biting. It reaches its apex when the Major visits the local newspaper to place an advertisement outlining his noseless plight, and the clerk refuses to co-operate, not because he's shocked by the meaninglessness of the request but in fear of a hidden significance.

> '...Enough false reports and rumours get past editorial already [...] Only last week there was a similar case. A clerk came here with an advertisement, just like you. It cost him two roubles seventy-three kopeks, and all he wanted to advertise was a runaway black poodle. And what do you think he was up to really? In the end we had a libel case on our hands – the poodle was meant as a satire on a government cashier.'

If any St Petersburg readers had assumed political innocence in Gogol's story, this passage surely would alert them to potential trickery. Is Gogol protecting his innocence in the face of a society which presumes even the most incidental of stories has a satirical intention? Not for me; this is more of a tease, akin to one of Shostakovich's doctored state-composed military themes, a sort of 'I couldn't possibly comment', though far less clichéd than that phrase, far more amusing, and far more obvious.

The veneer of jest in 'The Nose' also, of course, shrouds an underlying darkness. Alongside the suffocating and stifling nature of St Petersburg's nineteenth-century 'in crowd' is the very obvious tragedy of disfigurement. The prospect of facing a busy metropolis without one's nose, like the popular recurring dream of nakedness in a public space, conveys a very fundamental feeling of inadequacy and inevitable ridicule – ridicule that Gogol frequently received at the hands of *The Northern Bee*, a publication to which he directly refers in 'The Nose'. Also at the core of this story is the metropolis, specifically St Petersburg, whose walls and gilded domes have witnessed far more than their fair share of suffering and deprivation.

But the essence of 'The Nose' is surely its sense of fun. The central plot of nose-deprivation has both huge and tiny interpretative possibilities for those with a detailed knowledge of Russian culture and history, and also for those with none at all. Though even if you occasionally can't make sense of it all, it's enough to feel the episodic delight of the tale. As Gogol said, 'This world is full of the most outrageous nonsense'. Only the kind of fool who goes about the place without a nose could disagree with that.

A Sort of Healing

John McGahern, *The Barracks*
faber & faber, 2000

Bernadette Crowley

The Barracks (1963) is John McGahern's first novel. Set in Ireland in the early 1950s, it gives an account of sixteen months in the life of Elizabeth Reegan and her policeman husband. Four years before the story opens, Elizabeth has left her nursing job in England and returned to her Irish home. Hoping for love, companionship and, in her middle age, perhaps a child, she has married Reegan, a widower with three young children, and settled into domesticity in the police barracks of the title. 'And for a time she was happy, extremely happy at first.'

Elizabeth's life is not all she had hoped for. No child is born; her stepchildren accept her but not as a mother; and Reegan is difficult, moody and self-absorbed. Then Elizabeth discovers that she has cancer. She suspects this at the beginning of the story, eventually has it confirmed, undergoes major surgery, rallies for a while, and then dies. Reegan's great wish is to save enough money to leave his job and buy a small farm. He despises both the monotony of police work and the necessary subservience he must show to his superior officer, Superintendent Quirke. For Reegan, the job is an imprisonment. But Elizabeth too is held – by her marriage, her responsibilities, and finally by her illness – and the couple's individual struggles to reach a place of comfort is a metaphor for the larger world.

'What's all this living and dying about anyway, Elizabeth?' Elizabeth's English lover Michael Halliday had asked. But in this novel such questions are not easily answered. 'All answers are stupid and questions too,' Elizabeth tells herself at one point and then continues:

> I am pushing the bike because I am pushing because I am pushing. I am going home because I am going home because I am going home.

As often in McGahern's writing this passage exists on two levels. First there is Elizabeth's entirely understandable need to keep her thoughts away from the worrying suspicion of cancer – to keep them, as she puts it, 'light and musing and futile'. And then there is the directly connected larger idea that this gambit of evasiveness is not 'futile' at all. It is, McGahern would suggest, the dogged act of being that matters, and he demonstrates that human ability to move forward without any real grasp of the reason for the journey.

This is not an easy story to read. The big things – Elizabeth's ordeal after her operation and Reegan's clashes with Quirke – are almost savagely portrayed, while the smaller lives of Reegan's children are cut through with their own instances of pain. The quiet happiness of Christmas Day, for example, ends with the children being given a dose of liquid paraffin, 'the last taste of their day and it wasn't sweet'. But the novel is more than a commentary on the fleeting nature of happiness. Each episode of joy may be followed by one of difficulty, but by the same cycle, each difficulty must, at some point, give way to joy. 'O Jesus Christ, get me out of this fix. I can't stand it. God blast it! Blast it! Blast it!' Elizabeth cries during the dreadful aftermath of her operation. What eventually succeeds this, however, is completely beautiful:

> By the tenth day she could touch the back of her head with her hand and she had hours of happiness such as she never remembered.

Such realisations by Elizabeth are small enough to be achievable, and they bring feelings that save her from negativity. The cycle of joy and pain is reinforced at each stage of the story. The Joyful, the Sorrowful and the Glorious Mysteries of the Rosary that the family pray together each night are matched by the turning seasons: the endless cycles of liturgy and nature are expressions of the transformations possible in a human life.

Elizabeth's is the main story, but Reegan's runs alongside it, his oppressive and edgy conduct a contrast to her gentleness and compassion. Their lives are not acrimonious but they are lived separately. Again, though, there are saving occasions where a true connection is reached:

> And they were together here. It didn't have to mean anything more than that, it'd be sufficient for this night. She took his face between her hands, and kissed it softly, in gratitude. She was mindless now of all things, suffused through and through and lost in contentment, and in its gentleness and tiredness they fell into deep sleep together.

Such moments are, as Elizabeth realises, always transient, but still the fleeting gentleness has a quality of coherence. 'Lost in contentment' is another manifestation of the earlier 'hours of happiness', where each occasion is allowed to assume a type of perfection.

Elizabeth's death, when it happens, is bleak. Reegan is away from the barracks and she has been left in the care of the young step-daughter, Una. As Elizabeth's senses fade, the actual world around her seems to darken. 'But why did you draw the blinds?' she asks:

> 'What blinds?' the child was frightened.
> 'The blinds of the window.'
> 'No, there's no blinds down, but it'll not be long till it's brighter. The sun'll be round to this side of the house in an hour.'

Elizabeth's personal disconnections – from her husband, from her step-daughter, from life – are part of another severance. Up to this point it has been her consciousness that has dominated the narrative. But now, as she withdraws from the story, all insight fails so that any useful interpretation has to come from the reader. The child points to the movement of the earth round the sun – another example of the cyclical. Things will change, Una explains, 'in an hour'. Elizabeth, of course, has not got 'an hour' and it is a different darkness that she is experiencing. The reader, appreciating this irony, is saddened by it, but also accepts the lessening of tension and welcomes that movement that looks beyond the coming death towards something more bearable. The business with the blinds connects this part of the story with both the beginning of the book and its conclusion. 'Wasn't my blind down the first, Elizabeth?' the children cry in the opening sequence – an appeal to their stepmother to settle a small quarrel. The instance is repeated in the novel's closing paragraphs but here, with Elizabeth dead, the appeal is made to another. Death changes things, McGahern seems to be intimating, but not too much, and the repetitions of life provide a sort of healing.

This is a compelling novel. Elizabeth's desire to make sense of the life she is living is movingly portrayed; her relationship with Reegan is, in spite of all its problems, dignified by an underlying tenderness; and her acknowledgement of the delight that can be found in living emerges as a kind of triumph:

> There was such deep joy sometimes, joy itself lost in a passion of wonderment in which she and all things were lost. Nothing could be decided here. She was just passing through. She had come to life out of mystery and would return, it surrounded her life, it safely held it as if by hands; she'd return into that which she could not know; she'd be consumed at last in whatever meaning her life had.

Good Books

Have you read any good books recently? Tell us – answers on a postcard – about your all-time favourite book, a great book you've read recently or simply the book you're reading at the moment. Many thanks to Mary Knight and Ian H. for this issue's contributions.

Willa Cather, *My Antonia*

Mary Knight

Willa Cather writes about the lives of everyday people in the opening up of the American West, in a book that at once displays epic qualities and those of the domestic novel as written by Jane Austen.

Good Books,
The Reader,
19 Abercromby Square,
Liverpool,
L69 7ZG

Thomas Hardy, *Far From the Madding Crowd*

Ian H.

Starting with Bathsheba Everdene's refusal of marriage to farmer Gabriel Oak, Hardy takes his heroine from fierce independence to desperate subjection in her marriage to the headstrong soldier Troy. When his life is brought to an abrupt end by a third suitor – the solitary and morbidly intense Boldwood – Bathsheba turns once more, after a time, to Oak who has remained at her side.

There is much despair but in *Far from the Madding Crowd*, one of Hardy's brightest novels, the threat of loss is transcended by hope that overcomes malaise and misfortune.

Good Books,
The Reader,
19 Abercromby Square,
Liverpool,
L69 7ZG

Free Thinking

A Festival of Ideas for the Future

3–5 November 2006

Presented by BBC Radio 3 and BBC Radio Merseyside

In a series of live speech events and broadcasts in Liverpool, leading thinkers from the worlds of science, technology, arts and philosophy invite us to engage with ideas that prepare us for the future. The world of ideas today is rich, ambitious, boisterous, dangerous, interactive and interdisciplinary. The *Free Thinking* festival presents an opportunity to hear directly from thinkers themselves, and to question and challenge their theories: 'What is the future for the human body?'; 'Is the twenty-first century going to be "the lonely century"?'; 'Who does the new technology put in charge?'; 'Must we give up the idea of privacy?'

Free Thinking opens on Friday night with the live broadcast of the keynote lecture. Throughout the weekend there will be an exciting array of discussions, interviews, arguments and competitions centred on the Foundation for Arts and Creative Technology (FACT), and BBC's Radio Merseyside's new building, due to open later this year.

free thinking festival highlights

* A series of newly-commissioned dramas and fiction
* Live festival edition from Liverpool of 'The Verb', BBC Radio 3's showcase for new writing and speech performance
* 'Philosophy for Kids': special events for the thinkers of the future – children and teenagers
* Visitors to the live venue will be challenged with questions about where our world should be heading: 'Which thought of yours do you fear the most?' and 'Is being an individual all about me?'
* A *Free Thinking* blog project consisting of four blogs directed at different communities, from Tenantspin at the local level to a Delhi-based blog. Each will be hosted by an individual or small group who will stimulate and direct 'the 'conversation' around different themes and ideas connected with *Free Thinking*. Visit www.bbc.co.uk/radio3/freethinking/ from mid-July to watch the progress of this event in the months leading up to the festival
* The Reader will work with *Free Thinking* to help to bring Liverpool opinions and thought to light

Free Thinking: online, on air and live in Liverpool

Ask the Reader

Q Why aren't novels illustrated any longer? When I buy Victorian editions, pictures are part of the essential experience of reading them for me. But now neither new nor old fiction carries such aids to the imagination.

A I really don't know the answer though I suspect that it's more complicated than economics. We do know that the relation between writer and artist even in the heyday of Victorian illustration was often far from happy. Since the writer required the total attention of the reader, the visual image, which is always an interpretation of the text, was bound to seem an interference, as much as today do adaptations of famous novels for film or television. Contemporary illustrators seem to prefer the freedom offered by books for very young children where the words are simple and the stories brief and the opportunity for imaginative invention therefore freer. Even most dust jackets now carry non-committally abstract designs. There may even be an implication that illustration is not quite serious or quite grown-up. I remember the rather muddy photogravure reproductions of pictures by the likes of J. Barnard Davis and A. A. Dixon carried by Collins Classics and Nelson's Library early in the twentieth century and still to be found in every second-hand bookshop. They awakened curiosity in the young or unaccustomed reader to discover, on p. 356 or whatever reference the caption carried, the context that would explain the otherwise mysterious design. They were like a promise or reward to carry the mind through so many hundred pages of solid print. We expect readers not to need such encouragement today. Yet, I agree, there is an added delight in reading Trollope accompanied by the designs of Lynton Lamb or Joyce adorned by Robin Jacques.

The deeper reason must be I think that novels carry their own pictures within them and that the sense of the visual changes with the shifting identity of prose fiction. I don't mean simply that solid realism has been in the twentieth century transformed into personal vision, because the writing of George Eliot and Mrs Gaskell and Trollope involves an interpretation of the world as radically as does that of D. H. Lawrence or Virginia Woolf. It is rather that in the great realist writers the vision is engaged with a wider selection of the recognisable reality we all share, the world of things. The visual details in a novel by say Henry James or Conrad, on the other hand, are subject to a more extreme selectivity, specific to the range of meanings the book establishes. Illustrations in most modern novels would reduce such meaningful reference back into inert objects.

I'm looking at an old Collins edition of Hardy's *Under the Greenwood Tree* where Percy Graves, the illustrator, has wisely taken the most neutral scenes to depict, mainly to have an opportunity to show us Fancy Day, the heroine, though she looks slightly different in each picture. This is an intensely visual novel. Yet we start in the dark of a Christmas Eve with an unidentified man, actually the protagonist, making his way through a wood and recognising the different varieties of tree he's passing by the distinct sound each makes in the breeze. Only when he emerges into the starlight does he become visible, 'his profile appearing on the light background like the portrait of a gentleman in black cardboard'. He is joined by other members of the Mellstock choir, 'like some procession in Assyrian or Egyptian incised work'. In the uncertain light details appear in a strange order. 'Mr Penny's lower waistcoat buttons came first' and then when he looks round 'Two faint moons of light gleamed for an instant from the precincts of his eyes.' Our expectations of personal description are displaced by grotesque analogies with popular cut-outs of celebrities or the hieratic gestures of remotely ancient cultures or a man is seen in terms of a button and spectacles turned into heavenly satellites. Even in so early a novel, Hardy's distinctive visions of a world where human beings seem not to fit, to be both too big and too small, is realised in his description. So though, like you, I have a fancy for illustrations, let's be content with the 'pictures' the writers themselves offer us and admit that they often defeat visual representation.

> Except our loves at this noon stay,
> We shall new shadows make the other way
>
> John Donne, 'A Lecture Upon the Shadow'

subscribe

Make sure of your copy of *The Reader*
and enjoy big savings *
by taking out a **subscription**:

UK
p&p free

1 year	4 issues	**£24.00**
2 years	8 issues	**£38.00**
3 years	12 issues	**£57.00**

Abroad **
including p&p

1 year	4 issues	**£36.00 GBP**
2 years	8 issues	**£57.00 GBP**
3 years	12 issues	**£86.00 GBP**

Please make cheques payable to the University of Liverpool and post to **The Reader, 19 Abercromby Square, University of Liverpool, L69 7ZG**.

Include your name and address and specify the issue with which you would like your subscription to begin.

* Save 20% on 2- and 3-year subscriptions
** The easiest way to take out a subscription abroad is by using Paypal on our website: www.thereader.co.uk

Our Spy in NY

Enid Stubin

My own version of a Russian festival took place annually throughout a long tenure in graduate school. Crippled by writer's block and gifted in the wand'ring ways and slow of serial procrastination, I'd rummage through my bookshelves whenever a paper was due to find a fat paperback novel – *Anna Karenina*, in the since-discredited Rosemary Edmonds translation, was a favorite – and, instead of writing my paper, read the entire book over the course of a few days as if pursued. Something about Tolstoy, Dostoevsky, and Gogol made my own anxieties about the pains of composition recede into mindless irrelevance. The jovial Stiva Oblonsky, about to wreck his home in comfortable complacency, presented a more compelling prospect than my proposed essay on 'Skunk Hour' or *The Faerie Queen*. And it wasn't as if I were doing nothing, you know: I was reading Tolstoy. Or Dostoevsky. Or Gogol.

The Weissman School of Arts and Science at Baruch College recently presented a Russian Festival of art, film, music, poetry, and theatre, and I signed up for as many evenings as I could. The first event, a screening of the Grigori Kozintsev production of *King Lear*, adapted for the screen by Boris Pasternak, was shown in Mason Hall, the freezing Art Deco auditorium of the oldest building in the City University of New York. The film astonished me – the cadences of Russian iambic pentameter were both impenetrable and somehow familiar, and the actors, all strange to me, found dimensions in the characters I'd never seen in more recognizable portrayals. Lear's daughters defied Hollywood conventions and actually looked alike in the way that sisters do in real life, however much they resent, envy, and fear each other. The score by Shostakovich anchored the production in a seventeenth-century context while extending its relevance into timelessness. And the subtitles, well, were Shakespeare, which made for another level of recognition.

A week later I caught a staged reading of Chekhov's one-act 'vaudevilles,' translated by Carol Rocamora, in Engelman Recital Hall, a 174-seat wood-and-cinder-block theater two stories deep in the bedrock of Lexington Avenue. On the stage sat the director and five actors, vaguely familiar as off-off-Broadway regulars or members of the urban chorus in one of the *Law and Order* franchises, unremarkable in street clothes. But their work in three plays demonstrated just how gifted actors can inhabit a role and bring the world to life. In *The Bear*, a misogynistic creditor appears at the door of a wispy, grieving widow and is transformed by a thunderbolt of adoration and lust into a ravening lover. The next vaudeville, *On the Harmful Effects of Smoking*, features a prince of a henpecked husband who addresses his educator-wife's fundraising audience and subverts her cultural and financial project. Chekhov never completed *The Night Before the Trial*, 'A Farce in One Act,' but two Baruch students, Liana Tsirulnik and Alexei Matsaev, had written alternative endings, each performed that night to a delighted audience, and so gave a narrative twist to the ill-fated but hilarious love triangle at the core of the piece.

'An Evening of Russian Poetry,' also held in Engelman Recital Hall, brought together three American and four Russian poets, along with two translators, for a reading that transcended linguistic expectations and suggested the deeply collaborative nature of literary translation. Grace Schulman, Mark Strand, and Carol Muske-Dukes read translations of the works of Marina Tsvetayeva, Anna Akhmatova, and Joseph Brodsky, and Vladimir Gandelsman, Vera Pavlova, Irina Mashinskaya (Mashinski), and Julia Kunina brought us these works in the original. In the second 'act,' the Americans read their own poems and the Russians offered their translations of those works. And finally, the Russian poets read their own works in Russian, with the translators Richard Sieburth and Steven Seymour providing what were, Sieburth explained, 'adaptations': 'We call it an "adaptation" when we don't know enough Russian to call it a "translation".'

Immediately apparent was the regard and admiration all the poets had for the others' writing, although, struggling into my jacket at the end of the reading, I took in one of the translators' mockery of the Russian insistence that no Russian poem can be adequately captured in English. The other translator, who gallantly tipped some of his wine into my plastic cup at the reception afterward, provided me with no such insider's scoop but did insist that Pasternak's renderings of Shakespeare were some of the finest in the language. I bought a copy of Vera Pavlova's poems and asked the poet to sign it for me, something she did with graciousness and poise. The vibrant and vivacious Julia Kunina, who had organized the evening and read an astonishing 'Imitation of Boileau' by Elena Shvarts, gave me a copy of her poems and signed it to me while her husband, Dennis Slavin, endorsed me as 'a real pro' – my idea of an accolade. On my way home, I ran into the two translators in front of what has the distinction of being the worst Italian restaurant in New York City. Who'd chosen that joint, and why doesn't anybody listen to me? My first impulse was to greet them jovially, but a closer glance revealed them apparently ready to duke it out over Russian prosody.

Back at Engelman one week later, in 'An Evening of Theatre,' Debbie Saivetz directed the playwright Elizabeth Egloff's adaptations of two of Nikolai Gogol's most enduring works, 'The Nose' and 'The Overcoat'. The result was an uproarious pair of plays set in present-day New York City. Performed by Baruch students, faculty, and staff as staged readings with a minimum of props and sound effects, the two works conflated Gogol's nightmare world of mid-level civil-service prigs with a Manhattan populated by deliciously recognizable types. In *The Nose*, Kovalyov, a volatile tax assessor who has unaccountably misplaced his nose, encounters a range of local characters – his indolent and insolent servant, a truculent cabbie, a sententious senator ('I'm the speaker here; you're only the speakee'), and The Nose himself, tearing across the stage with a briefcase and miles to go before he sleeps. The resolution, forged in paranoia and conspiracy, nevertheless honors the poignancy and sweetness of Gogol's vision. The night's second offering, *The Sin of Akaki Akakiyevich*, presented a phantasmagoria of office politics, the External Revenue Service, and the psychobabble and marketing lingo of movie production and real estate, and established our hero as an existential figure 'Sans hair, sans teeth, sans – can you believe it? – coat.' I loved Egloff's loving reworkings of Gogol and the deeper resonances in her impish echoings of popular culture.

Having just gotten used to saying 'Russian' rather than 'Soviet,' I'm still not reconciled to the sociopolitical, let alone the aesthetic and artistic, implications of the breakup of the Soviet Union and the apparent quaintness of all things Russian to contemporary sensibilities. Jhumpa Lahiri's use of Gogol as a literary and moral touchstone in *The Namesake* speaks to this condition, the locus of human experience in Russian literature.

As I write this, old anxieties are kicking in at new deadlines looming – these days not a graduate-school paper but a column, a book proposal, a manuscript revision. And the glamorous distraction of the Kentucky Derby tomorrow beckons, along with an international film conference on naturalism organized by my buddies at school.

Then again, it's been a while since I've read *Dead Souls*.

Letters

Dear Editor,

I have read and re-read your editorial [in *Reader* 20] and tried to hold back from comment – alas, I have failed! I feel so sad that you dismiss the 'nature table' and the poem known as 'Daffodils'; your dismissal of both is interesting – and connected – I think.

Speaking from your 'rural school' I see your point that the 'dusty' objects on the nature table seemed like a 'punishment' but I was at an inner-city primary school in Liverpool – the same one my mother attended – and we felt proud to produce a fir cone, identify bird feathers or collect and name leaves from local parks (we had no gardens). The table was a little place of nature which we guarded jealously and added to with dignity. Like Billy Casper, in *A Kestrel for a Knave*, we 'escaped' in moments of sharing a world we couldn't enter; we were the grass in the pavement cracks.

The poem is the same. 'Familiarity has bred contempt', perhaps, but many of the students I teach recall learning to recite this deceptively simple poem of Wordsworth's and recall the music of the recitation with joy, not resentment. The enforced recitation was not ideal but it was, for many, a crack in the pavement, which years later they do not despise and 'in pensive mood' still use to translate themselves as the poet did.

I do not dislike the term 'nature poetry', no simple term would deter me from further investigation. Rather, it implies to me all that is natural and for many that was the 'dusty nature table' and the 'clichéd' poem. Like the children in Russell's *Our Day Out*, we would not have known how to apprehend nature but we could manage the table, our 'dance with the daffodils'!

Sue Garner Jones

And now good morrow to our waking souls,
Which watch not one another out of fear;
For love, all love of other sight controls,
And makes one little room an everywhere.

John Donne, 'The Good-Morrow'

The Reader Crossword

Cassandra No.14

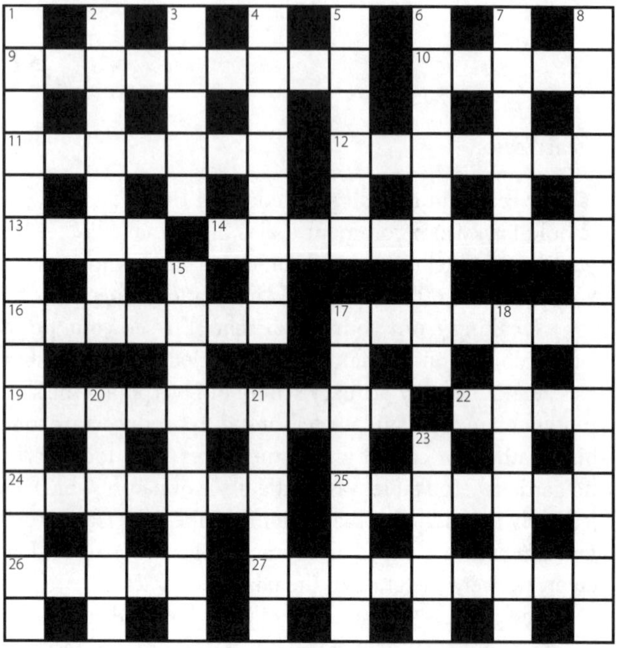

Across

9. According to Peter this leads inevitably to incompetence (9)
10. Is there cause to be embarrassed in having a bash at something? (5)
11. When to celebrate both Solomon's christening and the birth of a graceful child. (7)
***12 and 8 down.** Some distance from a scene of disturbance in Wessex (3, 4, 3, 7, 5)
13. Standard measure starts up north in Thirlmere (4)
14. Princess is found out of position (10)
16. Brass discovered in Europe's ETA survey (7)
17. Back in the mountain air, I breathe in the smell of this highly flavoured dish (7)
19. Considerate even when pensive? (10)
22. Complacent when mugs are substituted (4)
24. Nervously attributable to a wandering gait (7)
25. Ruler may be found in a foul temper, or perhaps not (7)
26. This African animal is all right with a circle's measurement (5)
27. Cockney intellectual shows sign of surprise when one of these is raised (2, 7)

Down

***1.** One of the top army brass? (3, 7, 5)
***2.** In this case the cures are desperate (8)
***3.** See 21 down
4. Swirling Lycra is caught in painter's medium (8)
5. Knockout view (6)
6. Sign of cereal on island (9)
7. Confused raptor may become household pet (6)
***8.** See 21 across
15. Perhaps showing special marks but not suffering from distorted images (9)
***17.** For our author these come two at a time (4,4)
18. Disarmer converts these enthusiastic fans (8)
20. Returning in part to reveal a vigour intrinsic to this form of arch (6)
***21 and 3 down.** Hasty letters do harm, circulating information about our author (6,5)
23. This field of battle is conjured up in our awareness of a ghostly presence (5)

* Clues with an asterisk have a common theme

Buck's Quiz 22

The Borrowers

From where have these authors borrowed the titles of their books and plays?

1. Howard Spring, *Fame is the Spur*
2. Noel Coward, *Blithe Spirit*
3. Aldous Huxley, *Antic Hay*
4. F. Scott Fitzgerald, *Tender is the Night*
5. Thomas Hardy, *Far From the Madding Crowd*
6. Margaret Drabble, *A Summer Birdcage*
7. E.M. Forster, *Where Angels Fear to Tread*
8. John Steinbeck, *The Grapes of Wrath*
9. Ernest Hemingway, *For Whom the Bell Tolls*
10. Iris Murdoch, *An Unofficial Rose*
11. Margaret Mitchell, *Gone With the Wind*
12. William Golding, *Darkness Visible*
13. Aldous Huxley, *Brave New World*
14. Dennis Potter, *Blue Remembered Hills*
15. G.B. Shaw, *Arms and the Man*
16. Frederick Forsyth, *The Dogs of War*
17. Brian Keenan, *An Evil Cradling*
18. John Steinbeck, *Of Mice and Men* (2 sources please)
19. Mary Webb, *Precious Bane*
20. Iris Murdoch, *The Sea, The Sea*

> Too high a price is asked for harmony; it's beyond our means to pay so much to enter. And so I hasten to give back my entrance ticket… It's not God I don't accept, Alyosha, only I most respectfully return Him the ticket.
>
> Dostoevsky, from *The Brothers Karamazov*

Contributors

Bernard Beatty is Senior Fellow in the School of English at the University of Liverpool. He has published several books on Byron and numerous articles on the Scriptures, Romanticism, Rochester and Dryden. He was editor of the *Byron Journal* from 1988 to 2005.

Josie Billington is an honorary fellow in the School of English at the University of Liverpool where she teaches Victorian literature. She is the author of *Faithful Realism* (2002).

Shelley Bridson is a child protection manager for Sefton Borough. She graduated from the part-time MA in Victorian literature at the University of Liverpool and continues to be a passionate reader who also writes poetry.

Sharon Connor is Schools Programme Manager for *The Reader* and a part-time PhD student researching Victorian literature.

Bernadette Crowley lives on the Wirral. Early retirement from teaching enabled her to study for an MA degree in Victorian literature at the University of Liverpool. She completed her PhD thesis last year.

Andrew Cunningham read English at Aberdeen and has a PhD on Hardy from Exeter University. He has taught English for eighteen years and is a former GCSE examiner.

Sasha Dugdale's second collection of poems *The Estate* will be published in 2007 by Carcanet/Oxford Poets. Her translations of Elena Shvarts' poems are due to be published in the same year by Bloodaxe.

Roz Goddard is a former poet laureate of Birmingham. Her first full collection, *How to Dismantle a Hotel Room*, will be published in October 2006.

Kate Keogan is a prize-winning poet and reviewer, currently working on a first collection of poems. She also translates Persian poetry and works as a freelance copy-editor.

Ed Kirk attends King Edward VII School in Sheffield. He has a Sheffield Wednesday season ticket and spends more time seeing his friends than doing school work.

Andrew Mellor is a musician and writer and regularly contributes to publications for the London Philharmonic Orchestra, the Orchestra of the Age of Enlightenment, Manchester Camerata, Symphony Hall Birmingham and The Anvil, Basingstoke.

Les Murray is a farmer's son and lives in a big dry Australian valley which he has come to resemble.

Adam Piette is Professor of English at the University of Sheffield. He is author of *Remembering and the Sound of Words* and *Imagination at War.*

Eileen Pollard is a third-year undergraduate studying English at the University of Liverpool and student volunteer at *The Reader*. She plans to start a research MA in September 2006 identifying influences on Virginia Woolf's *Orlando*.

Caroline Price is a violinist and teacher living in Kent. Her poems have been widely published in magazines and anthologies, and a third collection is due next year from Shoestring Press.

Len Rodberg received a PhD in theoretical physics from MIT in 1956. He now teaches and is chair in the Department of Urban Studies at Queens College, part of the City University of New York, where he also works on issues of health care reform in the United States.

Julie-ann Rowell's pamphlet *Convergence* was published by The Brodie Press in 2003 and was a Poetry Book Society recommendation. Her first full collection is due to be published this year.

Carol Rumens is currently Professor in Creative Writing at the University of Hull. Her most recent volume of poems is *Poems: 1968–2004* (Bloodaxe, 2004).

Myra Schneider's recent books are *Multiplying the Moon* (Enitharmon, 2004) and *Writing My Way Through Cancer*, a journal with poems (Jessica Kingsley, 2003). She is co-editor of an anthology of women's poetry, *Images of Women* (due autumn 2006).

Ann Stapleton is a freelance writer from Ohio whose work has appeared or is forthcoming in *The Dark Horse*, *Alaska Quarterly Review* and *The Weekly Standard.*

Enid Stubin is Assistant Professor of English at Kingsborough Community College of the City University of New York and Adjunct Professor of Humanities at New York University's School of Continuing and Professional Studies.

Rowan Williams is the Archbishop of Canterbury. His many publications include *The Wound of Knowledge* (1979), *Lost Icons: Reflections on Cultural Bereavement* (2000) and *Poems of Rowan Williams* (2002). His recent book on aesthetics, *Grace and Necessity,* was published in 2005.

Buck's Quiz 21

1. Antigone, *Sophocles* **2.** Beowulf **3.** 'Childe Roland to the Dark Tower Came' **4.** Satan, *Paradise Lost* **5.** *Il Filostrato*, Boccaccio **6.** Cleopatra **7.** 'Tristram and Iseult' **8.** *Romola*, George Eliot **9.** *The Birth of Venus*, Sarah Dunant **10.** *The Name of the Rose*, Umberto Eco **11.** Dante **12.** G. Chapman **13.** *Ivanhoe* **14.** King Arthur **15.** Ovid **16.** *I, Claudius* **17.** *Piers Plowman* **18.** Socrates **19.** Shelley, Ozymandias' tomb **20.** Tolkien

Please send your answers to Buck's Quiz, The Reader, 19 Abercromby Square, Liverpool L69 7ZG

Cassandra Crossword 13

Across

1. The acts **5.** Washtub **9.** Woolf **10.** Reflector **11.** Living the dream **13.** Long **14.** Botanist **17.** Oilfield **18.** Char **21.** By might or right **23.** Trains off **24.** Flush **25.** Satraps **26.** Between

Down

1. Town **2.** Emotional impact **3.** Coffin **4.** Shrugs **5.** Wifehood **6.** Stendhal **7.** To the lighthouse **8.** Barometers **12.** Bloodbaths **15.** Virginia **16.** Platoons **19.** Prefab **20.** Misfit **22.** Chin

Distribution Information

For trade orders in all territories except North America and Mexico, please contact:
Marston Book Services, PO Box 269, Abingdon, OX14 4YN, UK
Tel: +44 [0]1235 465 500 **Fax:** +44 [0]1235 465 555
Email: trade.order@marston.co.uk **Web:** www.marston.co.uk

For trade orders in North America and Mexico, please contact:
University of Chicago Press, 1427 East 60th Street, Chicago, Illinois 60637, USA
Tel: +1 800 621 2736 **Fax:** +1 800 621 8476
Email: custserv@press.uchicago.edu **Web:** www.press.uchicago.edu

For institutional subscriptions in all territories, please contact:
Sarah Preece, Subscriptions, Marston Book Services Ltd,
PO Box 269, Abingdon, Oxfordshire, OX14 4YN, UK
Tel: +44 [0]1235 465 537 **Email:** subscriptions@marston.co.uk

If you have any queries regarding trade orders or institutional subscriptions, please contact Janet Smith at Liverpool University Press on +44 [0]151 794 2233 or email janmar@liv.ac.uk